The Bombproof Roll and Beyond

The Bombproof Roll and Beyond

by Paul Dutky

Menasha Ridge Press
Birmingham, Alabama

Printed in the United States of America
Published by Menasha Ridge Press
First edition, sixth printing, 1999

Library of Congress Cataloging-in-Publication Data
Dutky, Paul, 1952-
        The bombproof roll and beyond / by Paul Dutky
            p. cm.
        Includes index.
        1. Kayaking. 2. White-water canoeing.   I. Title.
    GV783.D88   1993
    796.1'22--dc20   93-7348
                                                               CIP

ISBN 0-89732-085-9

Text design by Frank Logue
Cover design by Erin Wright
Cover photo © 1998 Brian Bailey/Tony Stone Images

Menasha Ridge Press
700 South 28th Street, Suite 206
Birmingham, Alabama 35233
(800) 247-9437
www.menasharidge.com

Table of Contents

Acknowledgements

My friends in the East Tennessee Whitewater Club helped get this project off the ground. Debbie Ashton, Paul Akers, and Diane Baldwin helped create a small video library that was used extensively as reference material for the illustrations, and helped us better understand paddle and hand eskimo rolls. Sam Suffern, Frank Modine, John Andriulli, and Gunar Leipins gave valuable input on the initial rough draft of the text. My thanks to them all, as well as to my sister, Sandra Brow, who helped proofread and edit my first draft.

I owe special thanks to Bryan Tooley of Sundance Expeditions in Oregon who spent several days in Eugene giving me an overview of the sweep roll as it is taught at Sundance. I alone am responsible for what is said in this book, but I owe to Bryan any success I have had in achieving my goal of representing both the brace and sweep rolls fairly and accurately as good whitewater techniques.

Creating the illustrations for this book proved to be a task far more difficult than anyone involved had anticipated. I offer thanks to Jan Atlee and Cynthia Cassell who helped create preliminary images contributing to the final artwork. I am deeply indebted to Marsha Nipper, my sister, who did a colossal amount of work on the first 120 pencil sketches, and edited a late version of the text. Thanks also to Sally Wiggins who helped bring several of my wayward attempts at perspective back on track. I am also grateful to Fonda Cloe and Mike Stoy for help with photography, and to Mike an extra thanks for his advice on lettering and inking.

When I had completed the first full set of illustrations, I asked for feedback from several experienced kayakers who could comment on the book's content and readability. This book has benefited immensely from their collective input. They are Teresa Gryder from Knoxville, Stan Stoy from St. Louis, and the following paddlers of the Washington Kayak Club: Carol Volk, Gary Korb (author of *A Paddler's Guide To The Olympic Peninsula*), Jennie Goldberg, Diane Troje, and Rick Williams.

Rick Williams deserves special mention since he commented on the manuscript and illustrations several times during their development, and added invaluable technical expertise to the chapters on playboating. Rick is a superb whitewater paddler and rodeo competitor, who has keen insight into how he controls his edges and uses balance, lean, and the paddle to routinely run Class V+ whitewater. Several of his insights were new to me, and immediately improved my playboating—I've passed them on to you, the reader, in this book.

Lastly, I want to thank those friends and acquaintances not mentioned here who at one time or another directly helped me with the book, or who won their points in the give and take of innumerable discussions of paddling technique.

Introduction

An expert kayaker makes difficult river maneuvers appear effortless. Little strength is wasted fighting the current; instead, the river's power is used to increase the boat's stability and help move it through the water. The paddle and the kayak itself are the two tools used to harness this energy, and of the two, the kayak is the primary one. As better boat control is learned, far less energy is expended on paddle strokes until a point is reached where the roll and many playboating maneuvers (like surfing, and playing in holes and on waves) can be performed without a paddle. The paddle is important, but it can only complement, and not replace, good boat-handling skills.

By good boat handling skills I mean the ability to hold the kayak level or on edge using knee pressure, to maintain balance using body lean, and when needed to shift weight forward or backward. These skills are fundamental to even simple maneuvers such as bracing, upstream ferries, and the Eskimo roll. The widespread inability of intermediate paddlers to balance and paddle with their boat on edge was an early motivation for writing this book.

The Bombproof Roll and Beyond is an introduction to edge control and balance for paddlers at the beginner through advanced levels. Most of this book is dedicated to the Eskimo roll, because the path leading toward mastery of the roll introduces the aspiring paddler to almost all the fundamentals needed for advanced whitewater maneuvers. A reliable roll also gives us the confidence to experiment with new techniques.

I'll describe several ways to roll, brace, and surf—a different approach from what many have experienced when learning kayaking basics. Knowing a diversity of techniques broadens your understanding of how best to manage the forces of gravity, buoyancy, and current that act on your kayak. Beginners are usually taught one "best way, which is really a collection of techniques chosen because they are easily taught to beginners. Limit yourself to one set of skills and you'll neglect many good, and more effective alternatives.

Some techniques presented in this book are simple, some technically difficult, and many only work in special circumstances—but all are worth knowing. An aggressive, skill-hungry attitude will open your eyes to more play opportunities on the river, and your enjoyment of whitewater will increase tremendously.

Part I of this book comprehensively describes the Eskimo roll, bracing techniques, and other skills that help you rotate and control the

■ Limit yourself to one set of skills and you'll neglect many good, and more effective, alternatives.

position of your boat's edges. The special use of the paddle to assist kayak rotation during the brace or roll is distinguished from paddle strokes that move a kayak across the surface of the water, such as forward, draw, and turning strokes. All the material presented in Part I can be learned and practiced in a pool or on flat water. I have left to others the task of describing basic strokes, eddy turns, and river-running strategy. Part II describes how the skills learned in Part I are applied on moving water, and introduces playboating techniques.

To represent accurately the lean and body positions discussed throughout the book, most figures in the illustrations were posed and photographed in my living room using video footage as a reference. The photographs were then made into pencil sketches, and the backgrounds drawn in around them. Kayakers are often drawn without flotation jackets or helmets on. This is done to show more clearly body position and lean—the reader should always wear a flotation jacket and helmet when kayaking.

Part I
▪ Bracing Techniques and the Eskimo Roll

1 · Equipment and Preliminary Skills

Mastering the skills described in this chapter will help you develop a confident attitude toward kayaking whether your boat is upright or upside down. It includes information on how to get out of a flipped kayak, how to pad and adjust the kayak for a snug fit, and how to roll your boat upright with some assistance. If you're familiar with these skills, you may want to skip ahead to chapter 2.

Everyone who sits in a kayak for the first time feels insecure. This is not only because a kayak feels tippy and frequently threatens to flip over, but because the lower half of your body is enveloped by the boat and then "sealed" in place by the spray skirt. The feeling of being trapped, of not being able to get out of the boat if it should flip over, may be overwhelming. That's why it's a good idea to practice getting out of a flipped kayak before learning anything else about the sport. When you know that you can easily get out of the boat if it should tip over, you'll feel much more relaxed.

This first "wet-exit" should be done with an experienced friend standing next to the boat. Tip yourself upside down and pause for a moment before pulling the spray skirt off the cockpit rim. Slowly and without hurry or panic do a forward roll as you push the boat forward off your legs, as shown in figure 1.1. If you need help, you can communicate to your friend by pounding the bottom of the boat with your hands, the paddler's universal sign of distress. Every wet-exit, of course, fills the boat with water that must be emptied. Avoiding this unpleasant chore is a great motivation for learning the Eskimo roll!

Equipment

River gear feels strange and bulky at first. The helmet, flotation jacket, and spray skirt often cause an initial feeling of claustrophobia. It takes several hours stroking across flat water before you use your paddle instinctively, maintain balance unconsciously, and wear your gear with comfort and familiarity.

Warm clothing is of special concern when learning to roll, because your muscles may not generate enough heat to keep you warm rolling a kayak bare-shouldered. Getting repeatedly soaked quickly becomes chilling even in the moderately warm water of a heated pool. A simple nylon spray jacket worn over a synthetic "pile" sweater may be all the additional protection you need to stay warm, but a dry suit or a wet suit

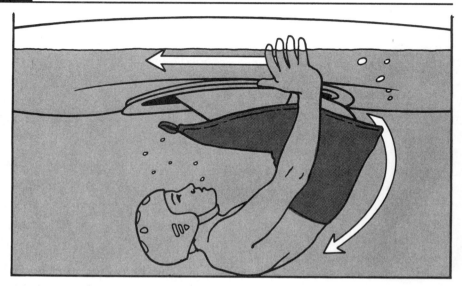

Figure 1.1: The "Wet Exit".

will usually do a better job. A wet suit permits a small amount of water to seep inside where it is warmed quickly by your body. You remain warm because the suits neoprene skin insulates this thin layer of water from the surrounding cold water. A dry suit keeps all water outside the suit by means of flexible latex rubber gaskets around your neck, arms, and legs. You stay warm the conventional way by wearing insulating long underwear and a pile sweater under the suit. If you use a wet suit, wear sleeveless shoulders (a "farmer john") in combination with a spray jacket or dry suit top to allow unrestricted shoulder movement. Becoming cold decreases the time you can spend in the water, and quickly turns fun into misery. Don't allow that to happen; dress warmly for roll practice.

Another discomfort when learning to roll is water pouring painfully into your sinuses. Learning to roll may initially be a slow and hesitant process. Unless you have the rare nose impervious to insult, nose clips or a SCUBA mask make the roll much more enjoyable to learn, and help you avoid a not-so-transient sinus condition.

The Kayak

Is using a certain type of kayak important when learning to roll? Not really, although some boats are easier to roll than others. It's not uncommon to see a boater Eskimo roll a 17 foot open *canoe*; be assured you can easily right any commercially available kayak with a good paddle roll. A paddler with a poor roll, however, may experience more difficulty rolling a boat with sharp edges than a boat with more rounded edges (a kayak's edges are also called its "rails"). There are many opinions about why this is so.

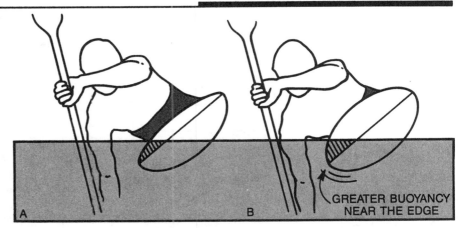

GREATER BUOYANCY NEAR THE EDGE

Figure 1.2 a, b: The off-balance kayaker in B receives greater support from his round-edged kayak than the boater in A receives from his sharp-edged boat. Most beginners would consider B the easier boat to roll. The difference in volume near the rail looks small in cross section, but can be substantial when you consider the additional buoyancy along the length of the boat.

I think it's because the greater air volume (buoyancy) at the outer edges of a rounded boat lends support to an inefficient or partially completed roll (see figure 1.2).

More important than your kayak's shape or volume is your ability to hold yourself securely in the boat. If your thigh/knee pads or hip pads fit too loosely, one of your legs may slip off its brace in turbulent water and cause an instant loss of control, or may cause you to fall out of the kayak's seat during a flip. Either event can lead to a swim. If the pads are too snug they may cause pain or prevent you from easily exiting your boat. Those kayakers who paddle in extreme river conditions generally prefer more thigh/knee and hip padding than do novices in order to maintain precise boat control.

Lots of padding, however, does nothing to keep you in the boat if you don't apply pressure to the foot braces, or if the braces are not adjusted properly. Remember that you hold yourself securely in the boat by pushing against the foot braces with the balls of your feet and simultaneously forcing your knees and thighs upward into the underside of the deck. Foot pressure, therefore, helps keep your bottom pressed firmly down into the seat and holds you securely in the cockpit.

Don't expect any fresh-off-the-shelf kayak to fit well; expect the opposite. Kayak seats often need to be padded in one or more places to get rid of painful pressure points, and thigh and hip pads should be individually tailored. Your knees should be comfortably held down and to the side, away from the center of the boat, as in figures 1.3 a and b. This knee position increases your leverage on the hull, and makes rolling the kayak or lifting it on edge easier. Taper down the front edge of your hip

▪ **Don't expect any fresh-off-the-shelf kayak to fit well; expect the opposite.**

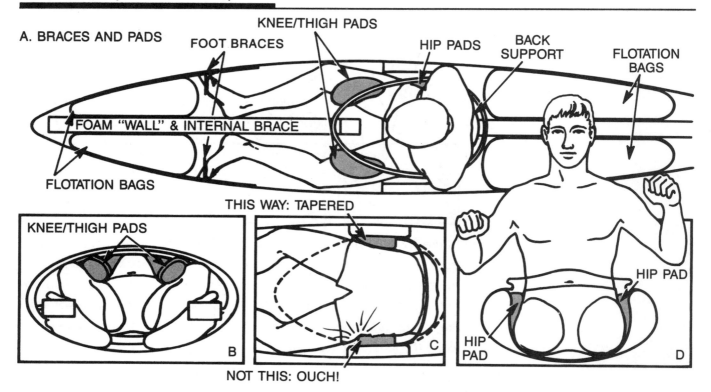

A. BRACES AND PADS

KNEE/THIGH PADS

FOOT BRACES

HIP PADS

BACK SUPPORT

FLOTATION BAGS

FOAM "WALL" & INTERNAL BRACE

FLOTATION BAGS

THIS WAY: TAPERED

KNEE/THIGH PADS

B

C

NOT THIS: OUCH!

HIP PAD

HIP PAD

D

Figure 1.3 a-d: Pad your kayak so that you fit securely and comfortably in the cockpit.

pads so they don't cut into your upper thigh muscles, as shown in figure 1.3 c. A low back support is often helpful and can be fashioned from a block of foam, a padded acrylic band, or a nylon sling. These are essential modifications that may take several hours. A loose fit will hurt your performance and decrease boat control. An uncomfortable fit may prevent you from paddling more than 20 or 30 minutes at a time because of skin, muscle, or joint pain. A borrowed boat should be outfitted like any other—bring plenty of duct tape and spare foam to the river when you borrow equipment!

While you're bent over looking at your boat's foot braces and knee pads, be sure it has a complete set of fully inflated flotation bags (usually two in front and two in back). A boat with full flotation holds less water than one with only partial or no flotation, is easier to pull to shore, and is much easier to empty.

Confidence Building: The Hipsnap and Eskimo Rescue

You'll gradually gain confidence being upside down in a kayak by trying the following exercises during a breaking-in period that should be painless and unpressured. Once you master these skills you can learn to roll comfortably.

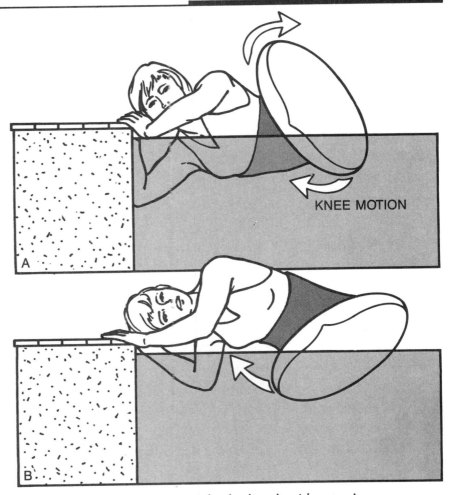

KNEE MOTION

Figure 1.4 a,b: A hipsnap can right the kayak without using arm or shoulder power.

Exercise 1. Place your hands on some support near water level (the edge of a pool) and, leaving your head at water level, alternately roll the boat upside down and right side up using your knees, hips, and trunk. This motion, shown in figure 1.4, is called a "hipsnap". Practice leaving your face in the water as you flip the boat up and down through several cycles.

Don't allow your boat to drift forward and away from the pool's side when learning to hipsnap. If you do, you'll find yourself leaning backward and stretching to hold onto the pool's edge, which makes the hipsnap much harder, and you may injure or dislocate your shoulder. *You are in control of where your boat moves.* Hold your head next to your hands and tighten your abdominal muscles to keep the bow of your boat pointed slightly toward the pool's edge.

Now is the time to check that you are not loose in the cockpit. A properly outfitted kayak will allow you to roll the boat upright confidently during the hipsnap. If you are not secure in the boat, you'll need to adjust the foot braces or do some additional customizing.

Exercise 2. Place your hands on another boat's bow and practice the

■ A properly outfitted kayak will allow you to confidently roll the boat upright during the hipsnap.

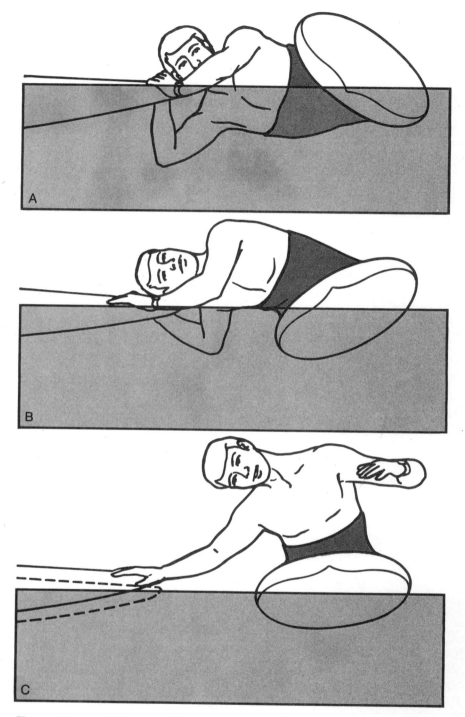

Figure 1.5 a-c: Sitting upright requires very little pressure on your hands as long as the kayak is rotated fully upright before your head is raised.

the same drill again. Keep your head close to your hands and do not lean forward or backward, as in figure 1.5 a and b. Pull your kayak completely underneath your body with your knees as you complete the hipsnap; *then* allow yourself to sit upright, as shown in figure 1.5 c. Your head should rise out of the water only *after* the rotating kayak forces it out of the water.

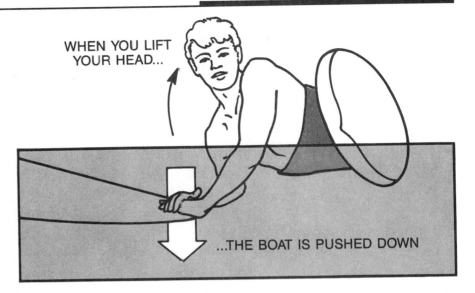

WHEN YOU LIFT YOUR HEAD...

...THE BOAT IS PUSHED DOWN

Figure 1.6: Poor Technique. If you raise your head too soon, your body weight will be supported mostly by your arms and not by the kayak—this method requires considerably more effort to roll upright.

The order is important. Always roll the boat upright with your hips *before* you raise your head and chest out of the water. This is much easier than trying to lift your head while the kayak is still on its side or upside down, as shown in figure 1.6. The upright kayak should support your body weight, not your arms.

During the hipsnap you can see how much work you're doing with your arms by looking at how far downward you push your helper's bow; ideally this should be no more than two or three inches. You'll place very little pressure on your hands if you use good technique, and should be able to hipsnap the boat and sit upright using only two fingers to support yourself.

Exercise 3. Completely submerge your head and body as your boat turns upside down, holding onto the other boat's bow with only one hand. Then lean upward, place both hands on the bow, lift your head to the surface next to your hands, and rotate the boat upright with your hips as in exercise 2. This does not need to be an abrupt motion. Keep your face in the water looking downward and think of pulling your knee toward your head. As the boat completes its rotation, your head rises out of the water naturally, with almost no effort on your part. Use your helper's bow as little as possible.

Exercise 4. Repeat exercise 3, but hang upside down for five seconds before leaning up to the surface and righting the boat. Progress to ten seconds, and then fifteen seconds.

Exercise 5. The last step in this progression of techniques is called the "Eskimo rescue," and is shown in figure 1.7. Turn upside down a short distance away from your rescue boat, and signal your need for

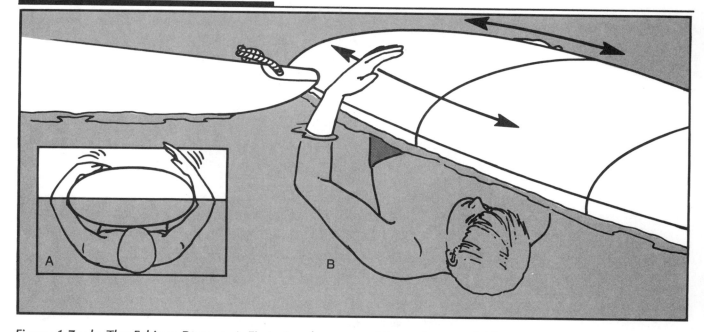

Figure 1.7 a,b: The Eskimo Rescue. A First, signal your need for assistance. B Then move your hands back and forth along both rails while awaiting rescue.

assistance by pounding on the bottom of your boat several times. Then actively move your hands back and forth along both your boat's edges so that you'll feel when the rescue boat arrives and on which side it is touching. Continually moving both hands allows your rescuer to contact your boat without smashing your hand or fingers, and with one hand you will find your rescuer's bow, regardless of on which side it contacts your boat. When you feel the other boat, pull your head to the surface and hipsnap upright. During an actual river rescue you should try to hold onto your paddle while moving your hands so you don't lose it.

The Eskimo rescue requires that you don't panic when you flip, which demands a good degree of self-assurance while you wait to be rescued. If you're comfortable with the Eskimo rescue, you're ready to experiment with brace strokes and the roll when paddling with assisting kayakers. You won't have to wet-exit your boat if your roll should fail.

The newcomer to paddling a kayak is often troubled by the squirrelly, tippy behavior of the beast. Although much of this ill-tempered conduct subsides after you and your kayak get used to each other, it usually requires a couple of years to remain upright in whitewater conditions without conscious effort. Unfortunately, during this period many paddlers develop an instinctive reliance on paddle brace strokes to keep them upright, instead of on good balance. This chapter will discuss how to use boat control and body lean to stay balanced, even in turbulent or choppy whitewater.

You can easily maintain your balance in a kayak on flat water (i.e., the pool) by sitting upright. Leaning sideways, however, moves your weight toward one side of the boat, which gives you a narrower base of support. Your balance becomes unstable when your weight shifts so far to the side that the kayak begins to roll upside down. The exact point at which balance is lost varies with the shape of the boat, the size of the paddler, and the effect of any current.

A useful, rough approximation is that you reach the "off-balance" point when your head is over the kayak's edge. If your head is above any part of the boat, you will usually be balanced; if your head is over the water, you will very likely be off-balance. When your boat tilts on edge, therefore, maintain balance by leaning into the kayak and keeping your head and as much of your body as possible over the boat. Let the boat support your weight, not the paddle.

■ Let the boat support your weight, not the paddle.

You can see how lean affects balance by experimenting with edge tilts next to the side of a pool or some other support. Sit rigidly upright in the boat (no side lean at all). Momentarily lean to the side far enough to tilt the boat up on edge, then gradually increase the boat's tilt, as in figure 2.1. How far does it tilt before you reach the off-balance point? Where is your head relative to the boat's edge? This off-balance position occurs frequently in whitewater if you sit too stiffly.

Now lift one knee to tilt the kayak on edge while leaning sideways toward that knee, as in figure 2.2. You may use one hand to help hold up the upper rail. How far can you tilt the boat on edge before losing your balance? Where is your head relative to the boat's edge?

You should find that you can maintain balance through the greatest edge tilt by leaning in toward the raised edge of your kayak. What you're actually doing is balancing on one edge of the boat. If you lean in tightly enough, the raised edge of your kayak will counterbalance the weight of your head and body. This takes a lot of effort on flat water, and is

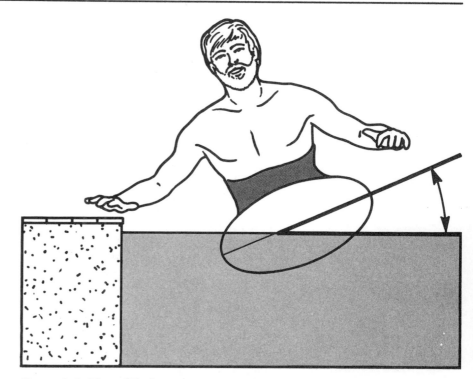

Figure 2.1: The off-balance position when sitting too stiffly.

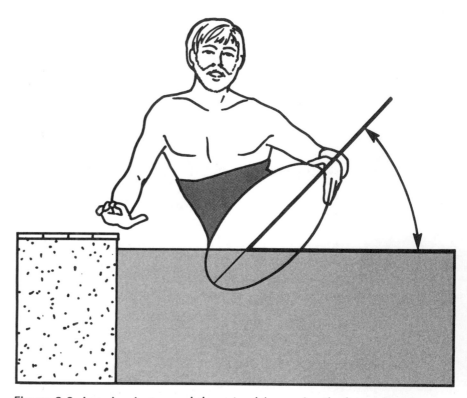

Figure 2.2: Leaning in toward the raised (upper) rail of your kayak permits balancing with much greater edge tilt.

especially difficult when you're holding a paddle and don't have a free hand to hold the upper rail.

This balancing act is much easier to do on the river where swells and waves tilt the boat on edge without your exerting any effort at all. "Leaning" in toward the boat on whitewater is simply a matter of *relaxing*, maintaining your upright posture while allowing the kayak's edges to tilt underneath you. This gives you the ability to stay balanced during the normal push and shove of whitewater without using paddle strokes. Absorb rolling and pitching motions, much like the rider of a horse absorbs the irregular motions of a horse's gait. An experienced paddler balancing in this way looks deceptively inactive, almost at rest, even as the kayak tilts and dips, obscured by foam and spray. The apparent lack of motion is illusory because the absorption of the ride takes place in the lower torso, but the ease of balance is real.

On whitewater, unlike flat water, you will often find it useful to change the edge tilt of your boat intentionally, and when playing in holes you may need to hold the boat on edge for a minute at a time. The muscle tone required to do this should be developed early, with the basic paddle strokes. Begin to include edge tilts in your warm-up exercises by holding first one edge and then the other off the water, as in figure 2.3 a. Next, balance with the kayak on edge and gently paddle forward, as in figure 2.3 b; then try paddling backward. Repeat the exercise holding the other edge up.

It is much more difficult to take paddle strokes on *both* the left *and* right sides of the boat while holding it continuously on one edge; however, this is far from being a trick maneuver. Competent river running and playboating often demand that you balance with your boat on edge and simultaneously reach over your raised rail to take paddle strokes.

Many if not most intermediate paddlers can't do this because they've learned to lean away from the boat *in order* to tilt it on edge. This misconception makes it impossible to reach over the raised edge of the boat with the paddle without dropping the boat's rail back into the water —a dangerous occurrence in whitewater where maintaining an edge tilt is what often keeps you upright. These paddlers quickly develop a phobia about reaching over the upper rail to take paddle strokes.

Avoid this misunderstanding of lean and balance. Learn to maintain a strong edge tilt using knee pressure to lift one rail, and use a lean *into* the boat to maintain balance. Which side of the boat you take a paddle stroke on then becomes a matter of choice. Intermediate paddlers who can confidently balance with their boat on edge should try paddling forward and backward *in a straight line* taking strokes on *both* sides of the boat, as shown in figure 2.4. It isn't easy, and feels awkward on flat

▪ Learn to maintain strong edge tilt using knee pressure to lift one rail, and use the lean *into* the boat to maintain balance.

LIFT KNEE AND LEAN TO
RAISE KAYAK EDGE.

LIFT

Figure 2.3 a,b: A Practice balancing with your boat on edge during your warm-up exercises—it's a skill as important as the basic paddle strokes. B Then paddle gently forward and back, still holding your boat on edge.

water. On whitewater, the current often helps to support your on-edge boat, and balancing takes much less effort.

These exercises require you to use muscles you may not have used before. The payoff is that the trunk strength and balance skills you acquire by holding your boat on edge enhance your ability to balance in rough water, in holes and on waves. You'll become less dependent on your paddle, and more able to relax. In addition, if you *are* thrown off-balance, a brace stroke may help you to regain balance. You'll find good edge control and lean make brace strokes more effective and easier to execute.

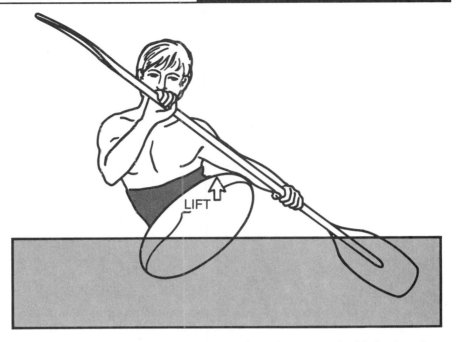

Figure 2.4: Work on your edge control until you can hold the kayak on edge and take paddle strokes on either side of the boat.

3 · Basic Bracing: Regaining Balance

Although with good boat control you can maintain balance under most conditions, sometimes you need a brace stroke to help keep the kayak upright. There is a similarity between basic brace strokes and the Eskimo roll. Both combine the use of edge control, lean, and the paddle; therefore, simple brace strokes are a good introduction to the Eskimo roll. Advanced, more difficult applications of brace strokes are skills best acquired after learning the Eskimo roll, and are addressed later, in chapter 9.

When bracing, the paddle serves the same purpose as the bow of another kayak did during the hipsnap practice in chapter 1: it provides momentary support ("purchase") on the water's surface that allows you to rotate the kayak back underneath your head using your trunk, hips, and knee pressure. A common beginner's error when bracing is pulling continually down on the paddle shaft and forgetting to hipsnap! This causes the paddle to sink deeply underwater, and is not an effective way to keep kayak and paddler upright.

There are three brace strokes (three ways of gaining paddle purchase) commonly used: the low brace, the high brace, and a variation on these, the sweep brace. In the descriptions that follow, the "outboard" hand refers to the hand farthest from the boat and nearest the blade bracing on the water. The "inboard" hand, closest to the boat, anchors the paddle shaft to your body, and so I often refer to it as the "anchor" hand, depending on whether I want to emphasize its position or its function.

The Low Brace

Do the low brace using the *backside* of the paddle blade against the water. Hold the shaft almost on the cockpit rim, and the blade as nearly parallel to the surface of the water as possible, as in figure 3.1. The low brace can be instantly applied because the blade contacts the water after only a slight tilt of the kayak.

Experiment with the low brace (and the other brace strokes in this chapter) by having an assistant stand just behind the cockpit and hold the boat on edge so that you are off-balance. Lean toward the upper rail to keep your head over the deck as much as possible, and then gently

Figure 3.1: The low brace with a gentle hipsnap.

hipsnap/ brace upright when the boat is released. Don't lean onto your paddle. Once you gain confidence in the support offered by your brace, you'll feel comfortable practicing on your own with gentle leans away from the kayak.

The High Brace

If the low brace proves inadequate to stabilize the boat, you can continue to brace by turning the power face of the blade (the side used for forward strokes) downward with a quick shift in wrist position. This changes your low brace into a high brace. Because the outboard hand holds the paddle blade near the surface as the boat rolls onto its side, the high brace can right the boat even when it has rolled nearly upside down. Brace upright with a hipsnap executed by pulling your lower knee strongly upward toward the bracing paddle blade, rolling the boat back underneath your body (figure 3.2). The high brace appears straightforward, but several important points need emphasis.

Blade Position: Hold the paddle where it offers the best purchase, perpendicular to the side of the kayak with the blade near the surface and parallel to it. Your inboard (anchor) hand holds the paddle shaft firmly next to your chest so that the power of the brace comes from the strong muscles of your trunk, and not the weaker muscles of your arms and shoulders. A hipsnap, with the paddle held in this position, can fully right the kayak without stressing your upper body.

Lean, Edge Control and Balance: Bracing requires little effort if you lean in tightly toward the kayak's upper rail as it tilts on edge. This side

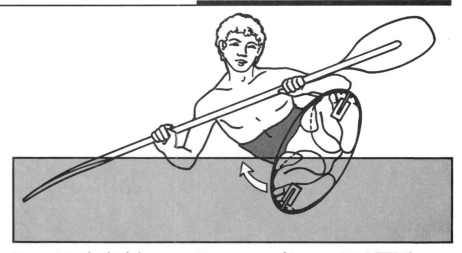

Figure 3.2: The high brace requires a strong hipsnap. Drive your lower knee up toward the bracing blade as you roll the kayak up underneath you.

lean keeps more weight over the kayak and less weight on the paddle. As the bracing paddle blade gains purchase, rotate the kayak upright using knee pressure during the hipsnap. The curve of your trunk naturally reverses itself from a tight "C" toward the upper rail, to a tight "C" toward

The WRONG way to high brace

A mistake common to beginners is high bracing with the anchor hand held directly *overhead* and away from the chest, as shown in figure 3.3 a. This "overhead brace" is ineffective and risky on flat water, and extremely dangerous in whitewater. The paddle moves into a position almost vertical to the water's surface, giving it little or no purchase. As the outboard blade dives the boat continues to roll over, turning an easy brace with a moderate edge tilt into an extreme high brace from an almost upside down boat (figure 3.3 b). As you fall into the water you could easily strain the shoulder supporting your bracing blade.

Your shoulder and arm are stressed further when you attempt to hipsnap upright. The hipsnap alone will seldom fully right the boat when you start with a deeply submerged blade, so the paddle is pulled through an arc underneath the kayak to complete the brace. Your shoulders, not your trunk muscles, assume most of this load since the paddle is not anchored to your chest. In the unlikely event that you do brace upright, you'll find yourself in an awkward, insecure final recovery position, as shown in figure 3.3 c. You'll find more detailed accounts of how the overhead brace increases your chance of shoulder injury in chapters 9 and 15.

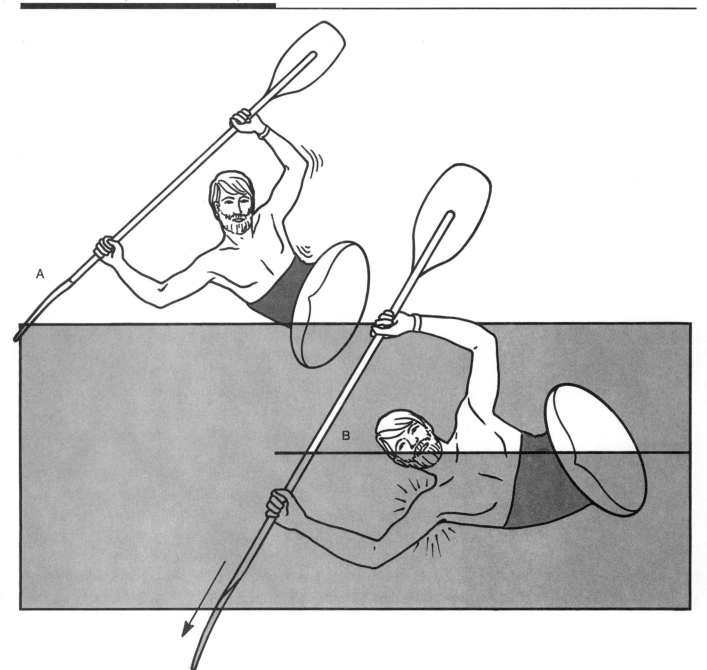

Figure 3.3 a,b: The WRONG way to high brace: A The anchor hand is held directly overhead, away from the chest. B The absence of a strong link between the paddle and your trunk places your shoulder at risk. The vertical paddle offers little purchase, so it rapidly sinks.

the lower rail as you complete the hipsnap and the kayak moves underneath you.

During the high brace, it may seem illogical not to pull the paddle strongly down into the water to push your head upward; but forcing the paddle deep into the water, or even raising your head higher out of the water will not obtain the objective you want. You want to rotate the kayak upright. I admit that your paddle will sink and you will "pull down" on it

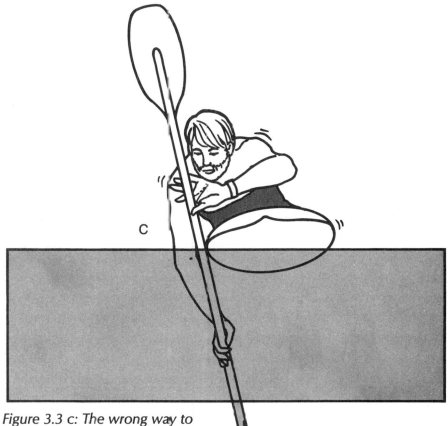

Figure 3.3 c: The wrong way to high brace: righting your boat after the outboard blade is deeply submerged may place a tremendous strain on your arm and shoulder, and leave you in an awkward position from which you can't immediately take a paddle stroke.

during the high brace, but this should happen as a result of doing the hipsnap. Braces and rolls will take the least amount of effort if you focus on hip rotation and knee pressure instead of pulling down on the paddle.

Practice the high brace equally on both sides with a friend standing by to help you with an Eskimo rescue if it's needed. Slowly lift one knee higher until the boat just begins to tip over, then brace and hipsnap by pulling your lower knee upward. Delay your hipsnap a little more each time to allow the kayak to tilt further off-balance before bracing upright. Practice until you can just get one shoulder or your face wet and still recover. If your high brace gets out of hand and you tip over, don't fight it! Allow the boat to roll upside down without stressing your shoulders. Before trying extreme edge tilts, first review the description of them in chapter 9.

The Sweep Brace

A sweep brace is performed by sweeping the paddle in an arc across the water with enough blade angle to keep it slicing to the surface. A forward sweep brace can be considered a horizontally moving high brace that uses the power face of the blade, as shown in figure 3.4 a. It begins near the bow and ends near the stern. A backward sweep brace can be considered a horizontally moving low brace that uses the backside of the blade, as in figure 3.4 b. It moves from stern to bow. A sweeping blade offers excellent purchase, and under some conditions (bracing on the upstream side of a hole) it's far more effective than a non-sweeping brace stroke.

Blade Position: The sweep must be brisk to give you good support, and is done using a quick rotation of the shoulders. Like the high and low brace strokes, the paddle shaft should be held as parallel to the surface of the water as possible by keeping the inboard hand low and near the

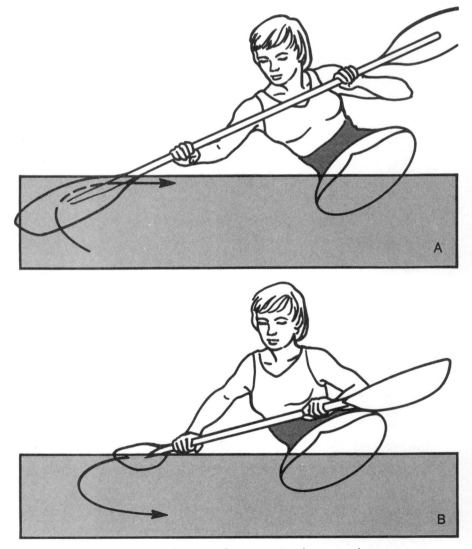

Figure 3.4 a,b: A *Forward sweep brace.* B *Back sweep brace.*

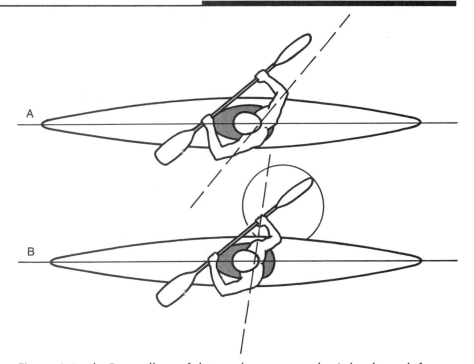

Figure 3.5 a,b: Regardless of the stroke you use—be it backward, forward, sweep, or rudder stroke—good shoulder rotation and relatively straight elbows as your blade passes behind the cockpit adds power and keeps the paddle safely in front of your shoulders. A Strong stroke: paddle blade stays in front of an imaginary line through your shoulders; power comes from your trunk muscles. B Weak stroke: your paddle is pulled behind an imaginary line through your shoulders; your shoulder joint must take the strain.

chest. The outboard blade should be angled so that it slices upward and remains on the surface. Play with changing the blade angle as you practice gentle leans and sweep brace recoveries, first with the forward sweep and then the back sweep. A very steep blade angle is part of a dandy turning stroke if your weight is over the kayak, it makes a poor sweep brace stroke. If you fall off-balance and weight the outboard blade, it gives poor purchase and rapidly sinks. A blade parallel to the surface (lacking any climbing angle) may dive under water as you sweep it away from the boat. Sweep braces help you develop a feel for blade angle.

Make sure that your sweeping paddle blade always remains in front of an imaginary line that runs through your shoulders. This should keep your arm slightly flexed, that is, your elbow will stay in front of your shoulders (see figure 3.5). If your blade gets behind this imaginary line, the result is a weaker stroke that could strain your shoulder. Use deliberate trunk and shoulder rotation to do sweep strokes correctly.

As you experiment with sweep strokes you'll find that a back sweep works particularly well when your kayak is not fully upright after a forward

■ Linking together your forward and back sweep strokes is an incredibly effective technique.

sweep. Linking together your forward and back sweep strokes is an incredibly effective technique, but requires a quick snap of the wrists to use the back side of the blade during the back sweep. Practice performing this movement smoothly and quickly.

Lean, Edge Control and Balance: The boat control used for a sweep brace is like that for a non-sweep brace: as you fall off-balance, keep as much weight over the kayak as possible by leaning into the boat. Hipsnap upright when your sweeping blade gains purchase.

Practice the sweep brace equally on both sides, just as you practiced the high brace. Slowly lift one knee higher until you can no longer keep your balance, then brace upright. Increase the level of difficulty by delaying your brace until you just get one shoulder wet. With large edge tilts you won't be able to sweep brace with shoulder rotation alone; a forward-to-back or back-to-front lean of your torso will keep the sweeping blade on the surface. Again, don't worry if you are unable to do difficult sweep braces at this stage. Chapter 9 describes advanced applications of brace strokes.

In chapters 1 and 2, I discussed how to "wear" your kayak, and how to remain balanced using only lean and edge control. In this chapter I described how to regain balance after it is lost using brace strokes. Once you've become familiar with the different brace techniques, you are prepared to understand and learn how to rotate the kayak upright after it has rolled completely upside down. I call any technique that enables you to achieve this result an Eskimo roll.

4 · Elements of the Eskimo Roll

There are many ways to roll a kayak upright safely and efficiently, just as there are many effective ways of doing a brace stroke. Any Eskimo roll is usefully categorized, like the brace strokes, by how the paddle is used to obtain purchase on the water. There are sweep rolls, brace rolls, and rolls that use no paddle at all, hands rolls. Because all roll techniques are subject to the same forces affecting boat rotation, it is not surprising that these different rolls have more similarities than differences. This chapter is about those elements of the Eskimo roll common to all approaches: the setup, the sweep, and the hipsnap/recovery. Each is discussed separately although they are often performed as one continuous motion. I'll describe specific roll techniques in chapters 5 and 6, and throughout the rest of the book.

The Setup

The setup position for a roll is a tight forward leaning posture with your paddle against one of the the kayak's rails and your face near that same side of the front deck. This low profile makes it less likely that you'll catch a rock as the current drives you and your boat downstream. Your helmet protects the back of your head, your flotation jacket protects your back, and the entire kayak shields your face (figure 4.1).

I suggest that you quickly tuck forward into the setup position when you realize you are about to tip over, even before your head gets wet. Besides the obvious safety considerations, a rapid forward lean creates momentum that will help carry you and your flotation jacket all the way under the boat. Your momentum and the buoyancy of your flotation jacket help to move your paddle toward the surface into a position from which you can begin the Eskimo roll. When a flip in turbulent water sends you tumbling, it's difficult to know which way is up, and a quick setup will help you become oriented more quickly to the surface again.

An Eskimo roll can be performed in a right- or left-handed manner, defined by the hand you use to sweep your blade away from the boat (the hand nearest the bow when in the usual setup position). I've used right-handed rolls in the illustrations, unless stated otherwise. In a right-handed roll, you set up by leaning forward toward the left deck and placing your paddle on the left side of the boat. The right hand (the hand nearest the

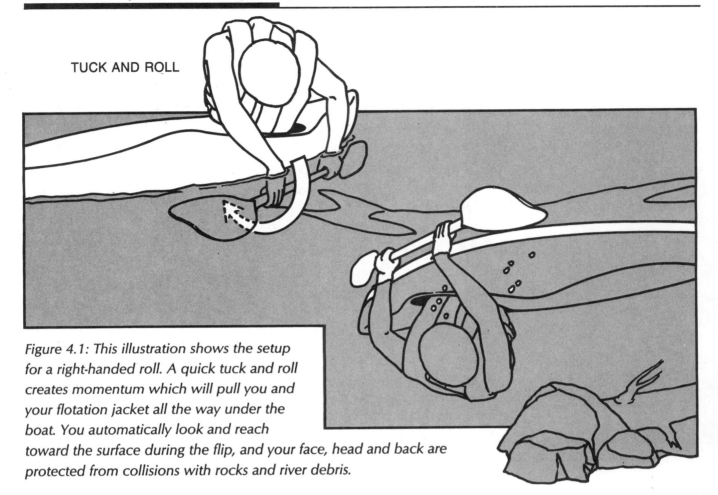

TUCK AND ROLL

Figure 4.1: This illustration shows the setup for a right-handed roll. A quick tuck and roll creates momentum which will pull you and your flotation jacket all the way under the boat. You automatically look and reach toward the surface during the flip, and your face, head and back are protected from collisions with rocks and river debris.

■ Having the paddle dive sharply underwater during the sweep is disastrous for your roll.

bow) sweeps away from the boat and becomes the outboard hand. The left hand stabilizes the paddle shaft near your chest and becomes the anchor, or inboard hand. The terms "outboard", "inboard," and "anchor" are useful because they make sense in describing either right- or left-handed rolls. The differences in the way right-handed and left-handed rolls are performed are described in chapter 7.

Control of the outboard blade angle is crucial to the roll. This blade should always have a climbing angle in the setup position so that as the blade sweeps away from the kayak it planes toward the surface. Most kayakers use a right-hand-control paddle, which means the paddle blades are offset 70 to 90 degrees, and you control blade angle with the right hand. This paddle is shown in all illustrations, and always requires a strongly flexed right wrist when setting up for any right-handed roll (as shown in figure 4.1). If you grip the paddle shaft too loosely, the climbing blade angle may be lost, and you risk having the blade dive sharply under water during the sweep—which is disastrous for your roll. *Grip the paddle firmly with your right hand.*

If you think that the paddle shaft has rotated in your hands, after your

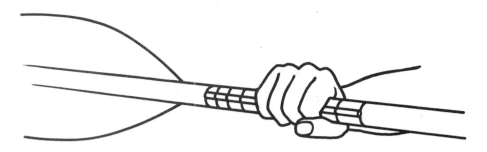

Figure 4.2: Nylon rope is used as a shaft orientation aid on this right-hand control paddle.

boat has flipped upside down, check the blade angle before you attempt to roll. There are many ways to do this. A short-term solution for a beginner is to tape a short length of nylon rope about ten inches long (or something of similar diameter) to the shaft of the paddle, as shown in figure 4.2. This ridge helps you easily find the power grip position, but it has the disadvantage that only one blade of the paddle can function as the right blade. (If a ridge was taped to both sides of the paddle, your left hand, which has to continually allow the shaft to rotate in a loosened grip, would become irritated.)

A better technique, which doesn't require any extra paraphernalia, is to slide your left hand down the left shaft until your long, ring, and little fingers lie on the throat of the blade, as in figure 4.3 a. Keeping your left wrist straight, rotate the shaft with your right hand until the straightened fingers of your left hand lie flush on the flat power face of the left blade (figure 4.3 b). This is the proper orientation for a right-hand-control paddle. Regrip the paddle shaft firmly with your right hand without changing blade position, and then regrip with the left (figure 4.3 c). You'll only need to reposition your paddle by feel when you're upside down, so work to make this maneuver instinctive, fast, and accurate. Whatever technique you choose, practice spinning and twirling the paddle in your hands with your eyes closed and then regrip it in the correct position.

An experienced whitewater paddler often sets up so fast that the kayak flips over and is rolled upright in one fluid motion; the momentum gained during the flip is used to help right the boat. However, I recommend a slow, methodical setup when learning to roll so that you can feel and accurately connect each independent movement. This is no place to take shortcuts; believe me, some patience here will pay off in the long run! First, become oriented to your boat when upside down by placing both wrists or forearms in contact with the side of the kayak. When at least one of your hands feels air or the paddle can be felt to move freely, you know the paddle is on and parallel to the water's surface. Like

▪ By using a slow, methodical setup when learning to roll, you can feel and accurately connect each independent movement.

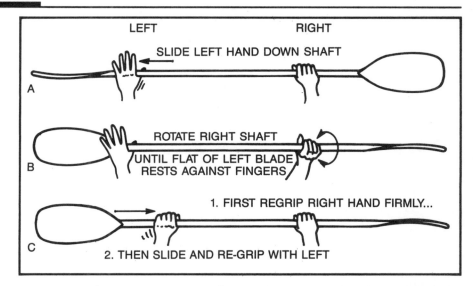

Figure 4.3 a,b,c: Regripping a right-hand control paddle by feel. A Slide left hand down shaft. B Rotate the right shaft until the flat of the left blade lies against you straightened fingers. C First regrip right hand firmly . . . then slide and regrip with your left hand.

a good tennis or golf stance and backswing, a good setup allows you to execute a technically good roll from the same position every time, with predictably good results.

The Sweep

The sweep phase of the roll is so named because the paddle, initially in a position parallel to and next to the boat, is swept away from the boat's side to gain purchase on the water. The manner in which the sweep is performed generally distinguishes one Eskimo roll from another, but in every case, the paddle blade should be held on or near the water's surface as the paddle is moved fully away from the boat. While the outboard paddle blade moves away from the boat, across the surface, the inboard paddle blade (and sometimes the inboard hand and elbow) moves over the kayak's hull, as shown in figure 4.4.

The sweep part of the roll sets the stage for rotating the kayak upright not only because the outboard blade moves to the surface at this time, but because your head and trunk move to the surface, also. The closer your head is to the surface throughout the sweep, the more nearly upright your kayak will be after the hipsnap. This is why leaning and reaching to the surface during the sweep is such an important part of performing a quick and effortless roll.

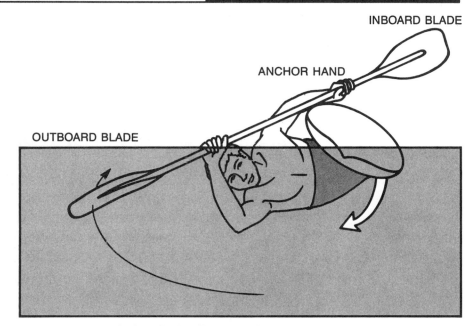

Figure 4.4: A right-handed roll during the sweep, but before the hipsnap.

Hipsnap (or Hip Rotation)

The hipsnap is almost a 180 degree shift in the position of the kayak's edges, accomplished by a complete reversal in the direction of lean. For instance, for a right-handed roll your torso leans all the way to the left at the beginning of the hipsnap and all the way to the right at the end, as shown in figures 4.4 and 4.5. Notice that the position of the paddle and upper body have not changed greatly. Boat rotation is driven by movement in the lower torso. This is true both for the brace roll described in chapter 6 and for the sweep roll described in chapter 5, but there are significant differences in timing. In the brace roll (similar to the high brace) the motion is abrupt, so that the paddle does not have enough time to displace water and sink. In the sweep roll, however, the hipsnap is diffused over most of the sweep stroke. The result is the same, but the motion is smoother, less forced than the word "snap" might imply.

The Recovery

Gravity must be overcome in order to raise your body and then your head from where they are floating in the water to where they are supported by the boat. To minimize the effect of gravity during the hipsnap (and decrease downward pressure on the paddle), allow your head and

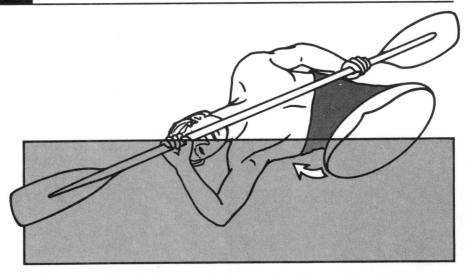

Figure 4.5: Just after the hipsnap. By comparing figures 4.4 and 4.5 you can see that boat rotation is due almost entirely to torso movement.

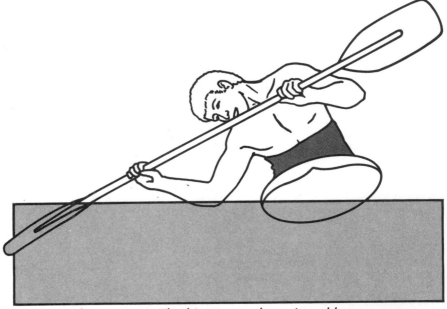

Figure 4.6: The recovery. The hipsnap and continued knee pressure pulls the kayak under your head. The paddle is not used to push your head upward and over your boat.

shoulders to stay in the water, supported by it, until the hipsnap is nearly complete. At that point the kayak is rapidly being pulled underneath you, and continuing boat rotation with steady knee pressure effortlessly rights the boat; the effect is like coasting upright. Moving your head the last few inches upward is coupled with the last few degrees of boat rotation, no separate, distinct movement of the paddle should be needed (figure 4.6). The rotating kayak will literally force your body out of the water as it rotates underneath.

That is the beauty of a good roll: if your face is the last part of your body to come out of the water, then the recovery, as a separate part of the roll, usually doesn't exist. The roll is complete and you are sitting upright over the boat at the completion of the hipsnap, ready to take a paddle stroke on either side of the boat.

Summary: Basic Principles of all Eskimo Rolls

1. Start each roll from the setup position.
2. Reach upward with your outboard hand during the sweep, and maintain a climbing blade angle to help keep your paddle near the surface.
3. Lean upward and move your head and trunk as close to the surface as possible as you sweep the outboard blade in a full arc away from the boat's side.
4. Begin the hipsnap after good purchase is obtained. Hipsnap (rotate) the kayak by pulling your knee up to the relatively stationary platform of your paddle, as opposed to pushing down on the paddle to raise your head prematurely.
5. Use head tilt and body lean to keep your head and torso in the water and supported by it until the kayak rotates underneath you, forcing you up and over the boat.
6. The "recovery" following the hipsnap results from doing the hipsnap and lean correctly. It is not a separate action of a well-performed roll.

5 · The Sweep Roll

There are hundreds of ways to roll a kayak, but only two ways to obtain purchase on the water with your paddle: one uses a sweeping, horizontally moving blade, the other a high bracing, vertically moving blade. While most rolls are a mixture of sweep and brace, all can be described in terms of these two pure forms. As it happens, many instructors on the West Coast teach a nearly pure sweep roll technique with a back lean upon completion, whereas many East Coast instructors teach a nearly pure brace roll completed with a side lean. Individual proponents of one roll or the other often feel strongly that their technique and method of teaching is best. I have tried to do justice to both types of roll, knowing that the techniques described here may not fully satisfy the disciples of either sect.

My attitude toward the Eskimo roll is quite open, which means I don't believe exclusively in one school of thought or the other. A comparison of the brace and sweep rolls is offered at the end of chapter 6, along with a brief review of my personal experience with each. A somewhat different roll, neither sweep nor brace, must often be used if you're trapped in the recirculating water of a hydraulic, which I discuss in chapters 12 and 15.

An Overview of the Sweep Roll

The right-hand sweep roll is detailed in figures 5.1 a-d. Begin from the usual setup position with flexed wrists. This wrist position is essential to give the paddle an initial climbing blade angle, and to keep it self-supporting as it smoothly sweeps away from the boat on the surface of the water. Unlock your wrists throughout the sweep to maintain the same slight climbing blade angle. Your head should stay near the surface and precede the paddle shaft as it moves away from the kayak. Initiate hip rotation at the beginning of the sweep and continue it throughout the roll. Lean slightly backward at completion of the roll, and tilt your head toward the water.

Bryan Tooley, an instructor and sweep roll advocate at Sundance kayak school in Oregon, has said that when the sweep is correctly performed the paddle blade slices through the water without any sensation of resistance. This makes sense because an almost flat blade angle gives the best paddle purchase for boat rotation, while you encounter the least amount of resistance to the sweeping blade. If not

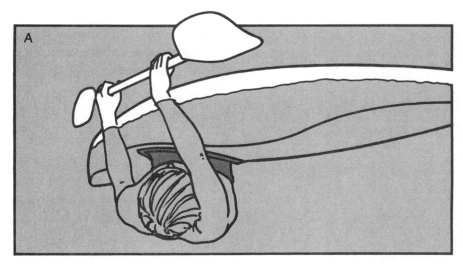

Figure 5.1 a: The Sweep Roll. The usual right-hand setup position with flexed wrists.

■ When the sweep roll is properly performed the paddle blade slices through the water without any sensation of resistance.

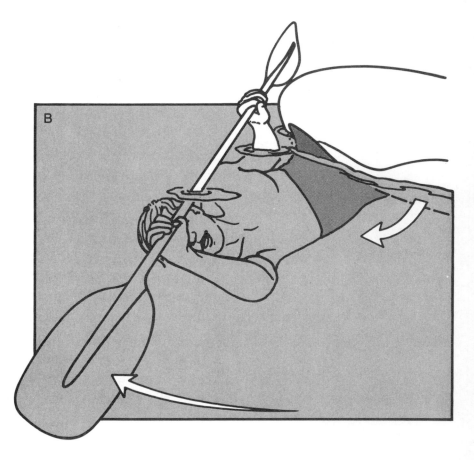

Figure 5.1 b: Hip rotation starts early with the beginning of head and paddle movement away from the kayak. Note the lean toward the surface, and the climbing angle of the outboard blade.

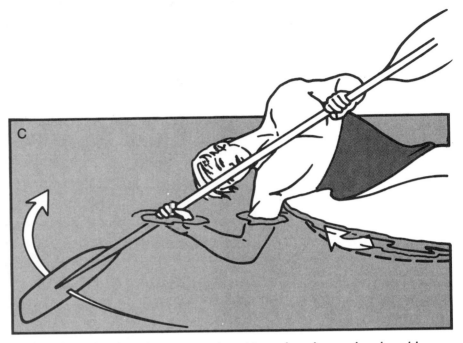

Figure 5.1 c: The head comes up last. Note that the anchor hand has been pulled in next to the chest.

Figure 5.1 d: The recovery (moving your head from a position over the water, to a position over the kayak) occurs as a consequence of the kayak rotating underneath the paddler.

enough blade angle is used the paddle will rapidly dive. If too much blade angle is used, water resistance to the sweep increases and the blade will sink, a phenomenon called "stalling the blade." If your blade stalls during a right-handed roll, the kayak tends to turn to the left instead of rotate.

You can get a good feel for changes in wrist position during the sweep while you are sitting on the ground in your kayak. First get in the setup position with your wrists firmly cocked, as in figure 5.2 a, the position you want to be in as the boat begins to turn over. Then sit up and place your paddle out to the side of the boat in the position you should be in at roll completion, as in figure 5.2 b. Move from the setup position to the roll completion position several times, and feel how your wrists smoothly uncock, just as they do during an actual roll.

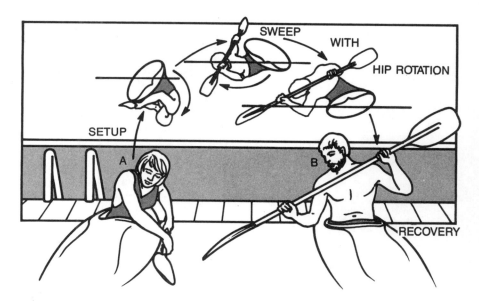

Figure 5.2 a,b: Sit on the floor and practice moving your paddle back and forth between setup (a) and recovery (b) positions—your wrists will move through the full range of motions they go through during the roll. As shown here for a right-handed roll, both wrists are flexed during the setup and finish and in a straightened position during the recovery.

A Method For Learning the Sweep Roll

The sweep roll, as I teach it, requires an assistant to guide you through the motion, preferably one who already knows how to roll. Each step in the learning sequence leads to greater independence, until you can roll without assistance. Continue to work on your form and timing until you can execute a technically perfect roll. A successful but labored roll is not enough; your ultimate goal is to roll upright easily and consistently.

The challenge in learning the sweep roll is that the sweep and hipsnap occur simultaneously. It is helpful to break the roll down into two parts. First learn to coordinate the hipsnap with your chest and head moving away from the boat (boat control), and then add paddle blade control to the motion.

Boat Control Exercises

1. **Hipsnap Practice**. Rest your hands on your assistant's hands and smoothly rotate the boat upright/upside down; you rotate the boat 180 degrees while fully reversing your side lean. Your assistant's hands should be a foot or so under water. Allow your body to float on the surface as you place only slight pressure on your hands. With the kayak upside down, your face will probably be just under water, unless you press down on your hands to lift your head to breathe.

Keep your head down during the hipsnap until the kayak rotates under you and forces your body out of the water. Your head comes up last and tilts toward the water, as if it were reluctant to be lifted upward. Continue the upward pull with your knee (rotating the boat underneath your body) until you are fully upright. Very little pressure will be placed on your assistant's hands if you do this correctly.

An educational exercise is to have your assistant support your hands at water level with your boat tilted 90 degrees and your head on the surface. Lift your head as shown in figure 5.3 a and observe which way your boat's edges move. Is your hipsnap aided or hindered by lifting your head? Does the boat start to roll upright or does it tend to roll upside down? Tilt your head toward the water, (figure 5.3 b), and make the same observations. It's always best to conquer your instinctive urge to lift your head for air. First roll the kayak upright with your hips—then breathe.

2. **Back Lean**. Begin practicing back lean by having your assistant hold the kayak in front of the cockpit and tilt it about 90 degrees on edge. Sit perpendicular to the cockpit, head resting on the water, as in figure 5.4 a. Then have your assistant forcibly move the kayak back into a level position. Allow your head to remain at water level, and lean backward (figure 5.4 b). This is really just a matter of relaxing and allowing the kayak to roll your head and torso up onto the stern deck. It is much more difficult for your assistant to rotate the kayak upright if you try to raise your head out of the water before leaning fully onto the back deck.

3. **Hipsnap With Full Torso Lean**. Now practice a full forward-to-back torso lean as you rotate the kayak upright with your hips and knees. Rest your hands on your assistant's hands at water level, and roll the kayak upside down as you lean forward toward the deck, as in figure 5.5 a. Move your head and trunk with your hands toward the stern deck as you rotate the boat upright (your assistant's hands move with you), as shown in figure 5.5 b. Concentrate on starting your hip rotation as soon

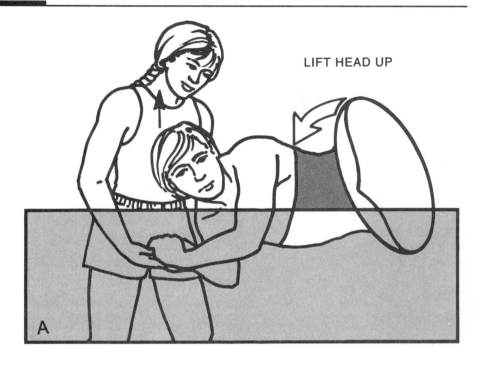

LIFT HEAD UP

A

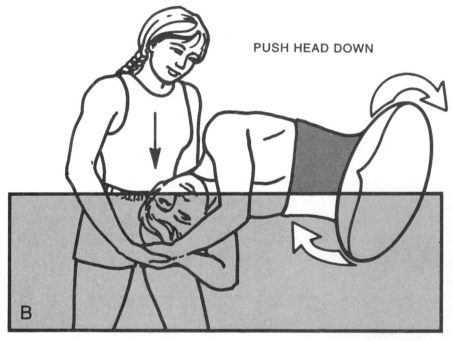

PUSH HEAD DOWN

B

Figure 5.3 a,b: Lifting your head prematurely destroys your hipsnap. Do this exercise and watch what happens to your boat's edges. Lift your head and you will unconsciously pull your upper rail in towards your chest. Push your head downward, and you will unconsciously pull your lower rail in toward your chest, assisting the rolling motion of the kayak.

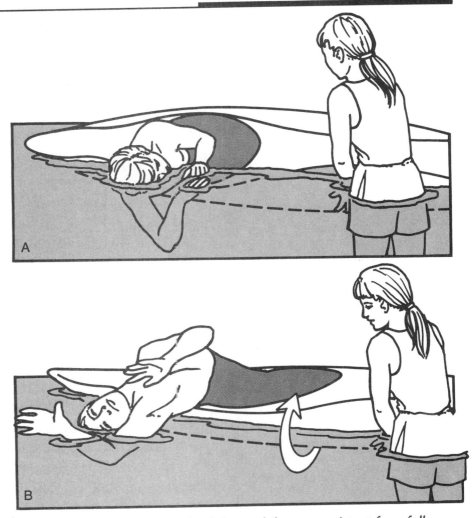

Figure 5.4 a,b: Relax into a back lean while your assistant forcefully rotates the kayak upright.

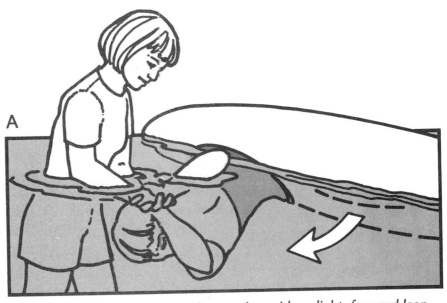

Figure 5.5 a: Hip rotation practice starting with a slight forward lean and ending with a back lean (see figure 5.5 b on the following page).

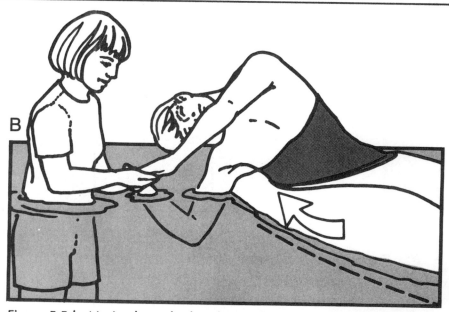

Figure 5.5 b: Notice how the head was tilted upward in figure 5.5 a on the previous page and downward at the end of the motion as shown here.

as your trunk begins to move away from the boat. This should allow you to rotate the boat well past 90 degrees before you pass the halfway point.

4. **Head Control And Hip Rotation Practice**. To keep yourself from raising your head prematurely, try using a rolled-up flotation jacket for support instead of your assistant's hands. Place your outboard hand in the center of the jacket, and your inboard hand on top of the first. Keep the jacket as far from the boat as you can for better purchase, and practice rotating the boat into the upright position, as shown in figures 5.6 a and b. Lean far backward during hip rotation to keep your head close to the water, and swing your inboard hand across the deck to the other side of the boat for balance. If you try to lift your head by pushing down on the flotation jacket you'll find it impossible to roll the kayak upright, as shown in figure 5.6 c. When you can perform this last exercise smoothly, you have learned most of the boat control and body motion necessary for the roll, and are ready to learn paddle blade control.

Blade Control Exercises

1. **Sweep With Lean**. While sitting upright, practice sweeping your blade in a large arc from the front to back deck, keeping the blade almost flush with the water. Then try leaning away from the boat as you repeat the maneuver. Your assistant can hold the cockpit rim on the opposite side to prevent the kayak from rolling over. This blade motion is your means of obtaining purchase during the roll, just as it is during a sweep brace.

2. **Sweep With Partial Roll**. Next, practice hip rotation and paddle motion together, with support from your assistant. Roll your

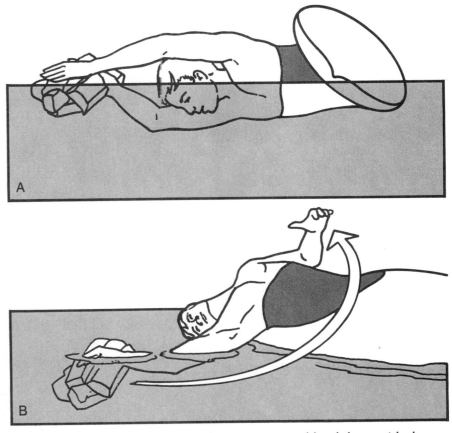

Figure 5.6 a,b: Practice blending hip rotation and back lean with the aide of a flotation jacket. Swing your free hand across your waist to the opposite side of the kayak to assist balance and help move your shoulders onto the stern deck. Notice how the head stays at water level throughout the maneuver.

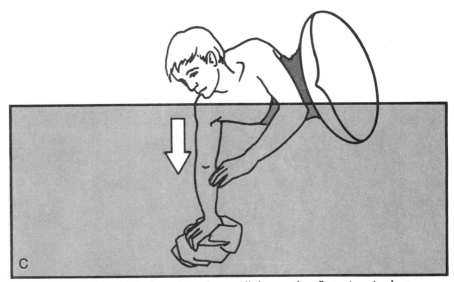

Figure 5.6 c: If you lift your head, you'll force the flotation jacket underwater and have trouble rolling the boat.

kayak upside down as far as it will go while your assistant helps keep your face out of the water by placing one hand under your armpit, as in figure 5.7 a. Then rotate the kayak upright with your hips while your assistant helps guide your paddle through the sweep, as seen in figure 5.7 b. I strongly recommend having your assistant support you under the armpit, as illustrated, rather than place a hand under your paddle blade. Supporting only the paddle causes you to lean heavily on it to keep your head raised. If your trunk is supported, you'll hold your paddle in position by pushing upwards with your hands. This method develops the correct body mechanics, and creates better habits.

To initiate this roll, first move your head away from the kayak keeping it as close as possible to the water's surface, and a moment later begin sweeping the paddle. Your anchor hand moves very little and fixes

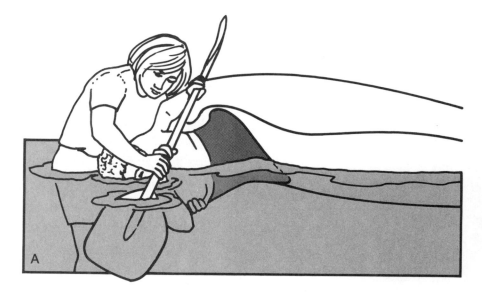

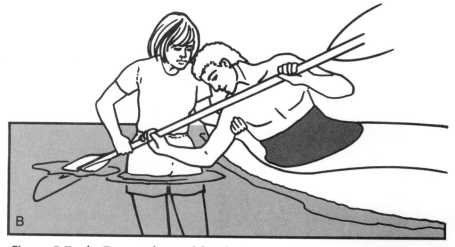

Figure 5.7 a,b: Dress rehearsal for the sweep roll: slowly perform the entire sweep roll with support from an assistant. As your familiarity with the overall motion increases and it is done more smoothly and quickly, your assistant will need to offer less and less support.

the paddle shaft near your chest. The power and stability of the sweep stroke comes from your trunk, not your arms. Begin to rotate the kayak upright as soon as you begin the sweep stroke. Near the end of the sweep tilt your head toward the water, look at your outboard blade, and pull firmly upward with your knee in order to pull the boat fully underneath you.

3. **Sweep With Full Roll**. Repeat the preceding exercise, but allow the kayak to turn further upside down, in increments, until you are starting from the normal setup position, with the kayak flat on the surface and your head underwater. Rely upon your assistant's support during each attempted roll until your timing and control allow you to roll upright on your own. Concentrate on one or more of the following points each time you begin the sweep roll from the fully upside down position:

A. Start from the setup position with your blade held at a climbing angle. If necessary, your assistant should correct your blade position before you sweep.

B. Do not allow your anchor hand to rise overhead at the end of hip rotation. Your inboard hand should anchor the paddle shaft to your chest and keep it nearly parallel to the water. If needed, place a small floating object (like a neoprene bootie or piece of foam rubber) in your armpit and attempt to hold it there during the roll. If you succeed in rolling upright while holding something under your anchor arm, you know you've kept it down throughout the hipsnap.

C. Take special care to move the paddle blade directly away from the kayak on the water's surface during the first few inches of movement. This is a backhand motion. Start the sweep stroke correctly, and it will tend to stay near the surface and give excellent paddle purchase.

If the inboard blade is crowded by the kayak's rail and bumps into the boat, start the sweep by first moving both hands, the entire paddle shaft, six to eight inches away from the kayak's side, as in figure 5.8 a. This will keep your anchor hand close to your chest, but give you more room to sweep the blade by initially moving it from a point near your waist to one nearer your shoulder. Another thing to try is raising your anchor hand several inches above the waters' surface just before the sweep, as shown in figure 5.8 b, to give the blade more room to move over the kayak's hull. As you finish the roll, your anchor hand moves naturally to its appropriate position next to your shoulder.

D. A good sweep need not be hurried, but it will not be effective if done too slowly; the paddle must be moving fast enough to offer purchase. Begin hip rotation immediately after you begin your sweep. Timing your hip rotation with your sweep quickly becomes a very natural movement.

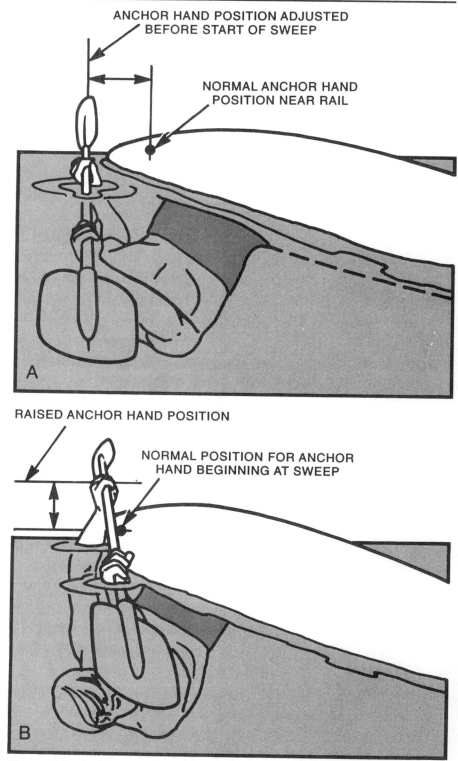

Figure 5.8 a,b: You can sometimes smooth out your sweep stroke by (A) moving your anchor hand sideways away from the boat's rail, or (B) raising it above the rail—just remember to bring it back toward your chest during hip rotation.

E. Complete the roll with a slight to moderate back lean. Do not sweep the paddle blade all the way to the stern where it has little purchase; stop your sweep while the blade is still well away from the kayak.

There is one good recourse left you if the kayak is not fully upright by the end of the sweep. A paddler who has mastered linking forward and backward sweep brace strokes can complete the roll by snapping both wrists over and using the back face of the blade to do a back sweep. This ability to extend your paddle brace stroke in order to complete a sweep roll is one of its real advantages in whitewater. Learn to use it by occasionally adding the back sweep after your roll, even if you are upright. Just remember that depending on a back sweep to finish your roll when practicing in the pool means you are compensating for a poor roll. Continue working on your roll until a back sweep is no longer necessary.

A well-executed sweep roll appears simple. The torso and paddle move smoothly in one direction throughout the roll. Hip rotation is so well diffused that it cannot be isolated from other movements occurring simultaneously. Coordinating the timing of each element (sweep speed, blade angle changes, hip rotation, and trunk movement) is not necessarily learned in one session, or even several sessions. The overall motion is complex. Be methodical, and familiarize yourself with each separate aspect of the roll before you put the movements together.

When you succeed with the sweep roll, continue to improve and fine-tune it. You do not have to do the sweep roll or any paddle roll perfectly to roll upright on flat water, but the adequacy of your roll cannot be judged on flat water. I managed to roll the first day I tried (many people do), but it took eight months of frequent paddling (and frequent rolling!) before I trusted my roll on whitewater. Some days it would work great, and other days it wouldn't. Roll often for practice in the pool and on the river between rapids. Have other paddlers spot you and critique your roll. A technically correct roll is almost always successful, and is worth striving for.

■ Depending on a back sweep to finish your roll when practicing in a pool means you are compensating for a poor roll.

The brace roll contrasts sharply with the sweep roll, especially with regard to the timing of the sweep and hipsnap. These are performed simultaneously in the sweep roll, but one distinctly follows the other in the brace roll. Since the hipsnap is not diffused throughout the brace roll, it is executed with explosive energy. Just as a baseball pitcher's wind-up prepares him for throwing a pitch, the sweep part of the brace roll brings the body into a tightly wound up posture from which it can be powerfully uncoiled during the hipsnap, as shown in figures 6.1 a,b. The rapid hipsnap completes the roll before the outboard blade has time to displace water and sink (figures 6.1 c,d). Energy is stored up and then released, in contrast to the sweep roll where the work of rolling is spread out evenly.

Paddlers being taught the brace roll are often told to hold their paddle in the air throughout the sweep stroke. This has the advantage of reducing the paddle's tendency to dive as it is pulled through the water: the paddler is forced to push up on the paddle during the sweep instead of pulling down on it. It also eliminates the problem of timing the hipsnap so that it immediately follows the sweep, which is difficult for some beginners. The paddle and boat are motionless at the end of the sweep, allowing the paddler to hipsnap whenever ready to do so (figure 6.2).

Although this approach is conceptually easy to understand and has some benefits, it is actually easier to sweep the paddle through the water. This is what the vast majority of brace rollers do after a season or two. I call the brace roll in which the paddle is swept through the air a "basic" brace roll, and one during which the paddle is pulled through the water an "advanced" brace roll. While the advanced brace roll has some advantages over the basic technique, it is useful to learn them both.

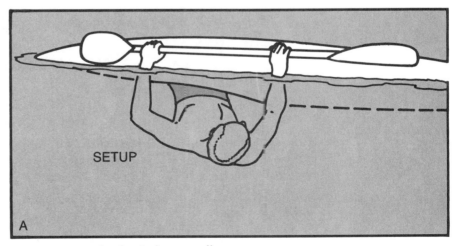

Figure 6.1 a: The basic brace roll setup.

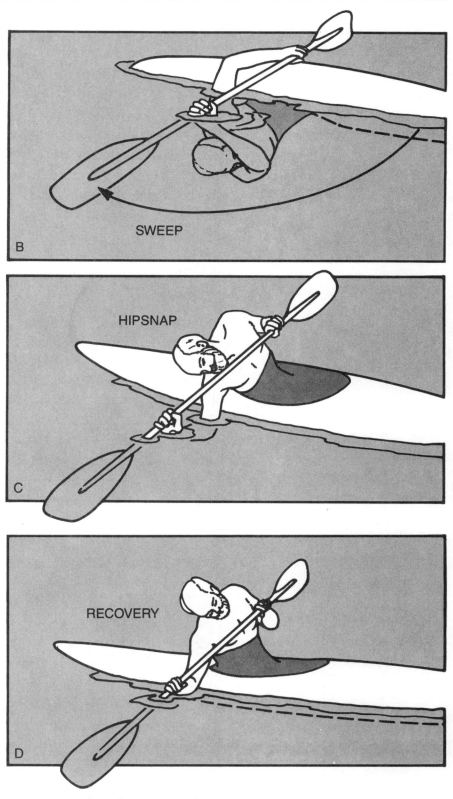

Figure 6.1 b-d: B *The sweep. The outboard blade is swept into a position on or near the surface and perpendicular to the kayak during the sweep.* C *The hipsnap strongly rotates the boat making it unnecessary to consciously pull the paddle downwards.* D *The recovery is simply a continuation of the hipsnap, a result of kayak rotation.*

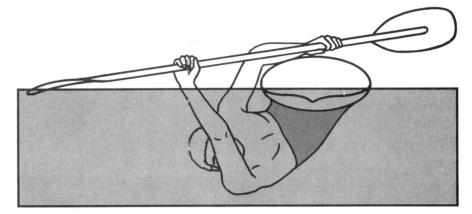

Figure 6.2: This is the high brace position, assumed immediately after the sweep stroke during a basic brace roll. No kayak rotation has occurred yet.

Overview of the Basic Brace Roll

The right-hand basic brace roll is detailed in figures 6.1 and 6.2. First, move the entire paddle through the air from the setup position (parallel and next to the boat) into a position perpendicular to the kayak. Hold the outboard blade on or near the surface by keeping your outboard arm in front of your face, straightening your elbow, and twisting your lower shoulder upward. While the outboard shoulder, arm, and hand lift the outboard blade, the inboard hand guides the inboard paddle shaft up and over the kayak's hull.

A powerful hipsnap rotates the kayak upright after the air-sweep. Although forceful, the hipsnap places little strain on your shoulders or arms because most of the work is done by chest, abdominal, and leg muscles. Begin the hipsnap by briefly shifting your weight entirely onto the paddle. Transferring your weight in this way means you "hang" from the support platform the paddle offers. It does *not* mean actively pulling down on the paddle shaft. Hipsnap as you "unweight" the kayak and drive your right knee up toward the paddle, which momentarily remains on the surface.

▪ The hipsnap will rotate the boat fully upright if you don't interfere with that motion once it has begun.

The hipsnap will rotate the boat fully upright if you don't interfere with that motion once it has begun. *Keep your head down* until the boat's cockpit rim pushes into your ribs, forcing your head and torso out of the water. It may help to tilt your head toward your outboard paddle blade and look at it during the hipsnap (figure 6.1 c). Raising your head too soon can abruptly stop boat rotation, because to support this movement you will unconsciously pull the rail of the kayak that is in the air toward you with your knee.

Balance is regained when the kayak rotates back underneath your body. A side lean, with just a little back lean to bring the paddle shaft into line with your hips, is probably the strongest position from which to complete the roll, and leaves you with a good view of the river upon rolling upright. A full forward lean or a full back lean during the hipsnap also results in a technically good brace roll, but I don't think the final recovery position is as good as with a side lean.

A Method For Learning the Basic Brace Roll

Boat Control Exercises

Exercise 1. **Practice Hipsnap and Lean Without a Paddle**. This exercise is a repetition of the first exercise described for learning the sweep roll. To summarize, rest your hands on those of your assistant at water level, and hipsnap the kayak upright using a strong side lean to keep your head in or near the water until the hipsnap has been completed. The hipsnap is a confident, smooth, unbroken motion. Upon completion you should be upright without any pressure remaining on your assistant's hands.

Exercise 2. **Tuck and Roll**. This exercise, shown in figure 6.3, helps you learn to extend your body away from the boat and remain oriented to the surface. Roll upside down away from your assistant in the tucked-forward setup position without the paddle. Then lean upward and away from the kayak, slide both of your hands onto the waiting hands of your assistant, and hipsnap upright as described in exercise 1.

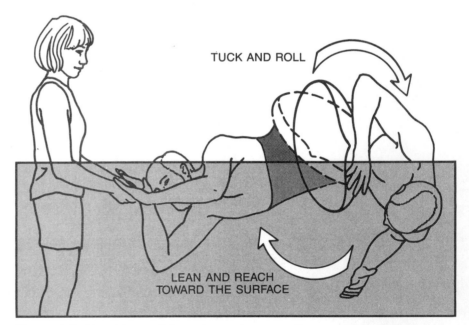

Figure 6.3: Combine roll into the water away from your assistant with an upward lean, then a hipsnap. This should smooth out the body mechanics of the brace roll and improve your orientation to the surface.

Exercise 3. **Head Control and Hipsnap Practice With a Flotation Jacket**. To cure yourself from raising your head prematurely, use a rolled up flotation jacket for support instead of your assistant's hands, in a fashion similar to that used for the sweep roll in figure 5.6. This time, however, *lean far forward or to the side* as you complete the hipsnap. Keep your head close to the water, and swing your free hand across the bow of the boat for better balance. The flotation jacket will offer the best support if you stretch to keep it as far away from the kayak's side as possible. This is exceptional practice for learning any kind of roll, because it shows you that only slight pressure on your hands (or paddle) is really needed if you keep your head down and roll the kayak with your knees and hips.

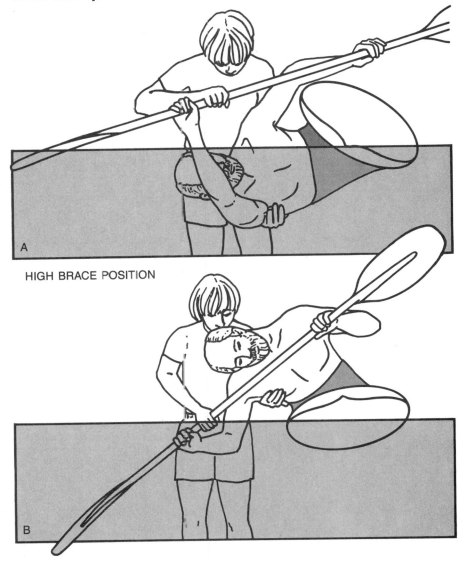

HIGH BRACE POSITION

Figure 6.4 a,b: Have your assistant help you practice the hipsnap from the highbrace position by supporting your trunk and paddle.

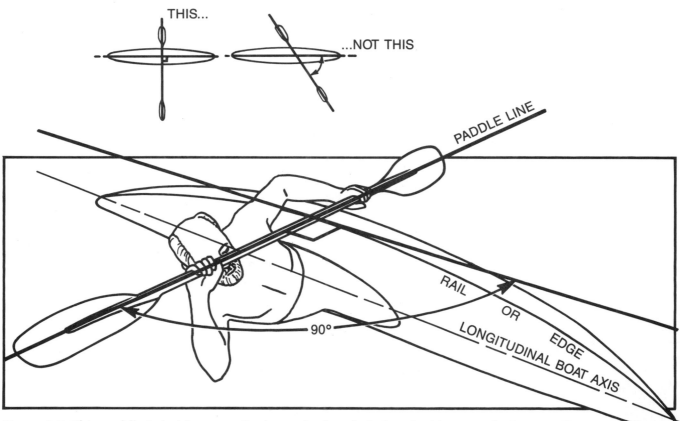

Figure 6.5: This paddle is held perpendicular to the kayak during the hipsnap of a brace roll.

Blade Control Exercises

Exercise 1. **Explore the High Brace Position**. Have your assistant tilt the kayak 90 degrees on its side while supporting your trunk with one hand under your armpit (so that your face remains out of the water). Move your paddle and trunk into the high brace position and hipsnap upright. Figure 6.4 shows this exercise with the boat held at an angle of about 45 degrees. Each time you repeat the exercise, have your assistant incrementally increase the kayak's starting tilt. As you approach the full upside down position you must assume a marked side lean. Your inboard forearm will slide farther up onto the hull of the kayak until you reach the position shown in figure 6.2.

Exercise 2. **Keep Your Paddle Perpendicular to the Kayak Throughout the Hipsnap.** The paddle should be held at right angles to the kayak throughout the hipsnap, as shown in figure 6.5. You can practice holding your hands (and the paddle) in the 90 degree plane by having your assistant hold your paddle securely with both hands to prevent any swinging of the shaft, as shown in figure 6.6 a. Your outboard blade should be held about a foot underwater. Roll upside down and slowly (at first) hipsnap upright. Observe your hand and arm position at

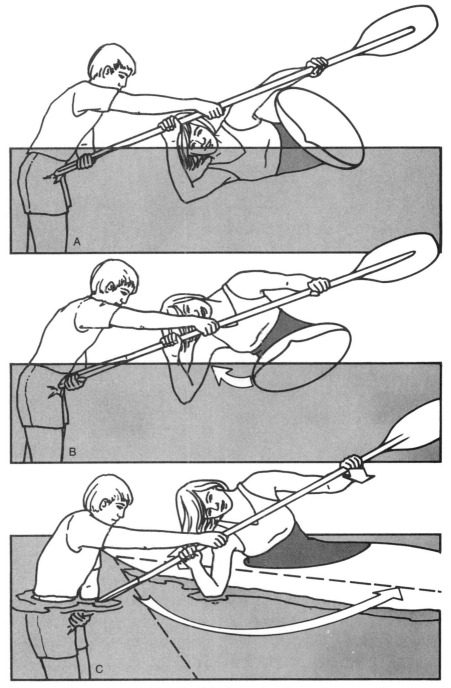

Figure 6.6 a,b: This exercise will help you to keep your paddle perpendicular to the kayak throughout the hipsnap. C Wrong way. Pulling the outboard hand backward, or pushing the inboard hand forward, will cause the boat to turn—both arm motions are harmful to your brace roll.

the completion of the hipsnap (figure 6.6 b). If you keep your hands in the 90 degree plane, the kayak won't turn or move forward, it will only rotate. If you fail to hold the paddle perpendicular to the kayak and instead pull it backward, the boat will move forward and turn away from your assistant (figure 6.6 c).

Exercise 3. **Keep Your Anchor Hand Low Throughout the Hipsnap**. The inboard paddle shaft is forced upward in mid roll as the kayak's rail rises out of the water, and your inboard hand, held just above the rail, rises with it. If it is not brought back to your chest as the kayak rotates upright (*anchoring* the paddle to your chest), it may rise all the way overhead, resulting in a nearly vertical paddle position. Failure to lower the anchor hand is a common problem with the brace roll. Keep your anchor hand low by drawing your inboard arm and bent elbow to your side as you complete the hipsnap, as shown in figure 6.6 b. The more parallel to the surface you keep your paddle shaft, the better purchase you're likely to have, and the more efficient your roll.

Learning Each Element of the Roll in Sequence

The preceding exercises help you to perform each separate element of the brace roll effectively. The next challenge is to link them together smoothly. Have your assistant guide you through the complete brace roll by supporting you under your outboard arm, as in figure 6.4. Place careful emphasis on your setup blade position. When you master this, have your helper assist only with the sweep and hipsnap, and finally only with the hipsnap. Support under your outboard arm should be gradually withdrawn until you do the roll on your own.

Exercise 1. **The Setup**. Lean forward into the setup position and roll upside down. Your forearms should be against the boat, the paddle parallel to the boat, and your hands out of the water. Initially flexing both wrists when doing right-hand rolls, will give the blade a climbing angle. It will not catch or dive into the water during the sweep. Your assistant corrects the position of your paddle, if necessary, and then with one hand under your armpit for support and the other on your paddle shaft, guides you through the sweep stroke. *Move slowly*, to retain an awareness of body, wrist and arm position. The more familiar you become with these movements, the faster you will do them.

When you're in good position, your assistant taps on the bottom of the boat to signal you to hipsnap the boat upright. Your assistant should use the hand that was guiding the paddle to tap the boat, so that you remain supported under your trunk.

Exercise 2. **The Sweep**. Set up on your own, and slowly sweep the paddle with guidance from your assistant. Your wrists should straighten, and the outboard blade should rest flat on the water's surface as the paddle reaches 90 degrees. While you hold your inboard hand over the kayak's hull, move your outboard arm in front of your face in order to hold the paddle blade on the surface. Your head and torso move just before your sweep begins; feel the position your body assumes as you lean toward the surface.

Your assistant should correct your paddle blade position if necessary, and make sure your trunk and paddle shaft are perpendicular to the kayak after the sweep, as in figure 6.5. When you receive the signal to hipsnap, try to use only knee pressure and a reversal in body lean to roll upright.

Exercise 3. **The Hipsnap**. After the setup, sweep and hipsnap on your own with the assistant giving only enough support to ensure the roll is completed. This may be done by supporting your chest, supporting the outboard paddle blade, or by assisting boat rotation with gentle hand pressure on the stern. To roll successfully, the hipsnap must be brisk. Keep your face down by looking at the paddle blade throughout the hipsnap, and remember to lower your inboard hand.

Exercise 4. **Perfecting Paddle and Blade Position**. When you can roll upright on your own, congratulations! At the risk of dampening your enthusiasm, however, remember that the large surface area of a paddle allows you to roll upright with even poor paddle blade control. Many people never improve their roll once they manage to once roll upright on flat water. Don't make that mistake, or you'll regret it when you find you can't consistently roll upright on whitewater. Before you

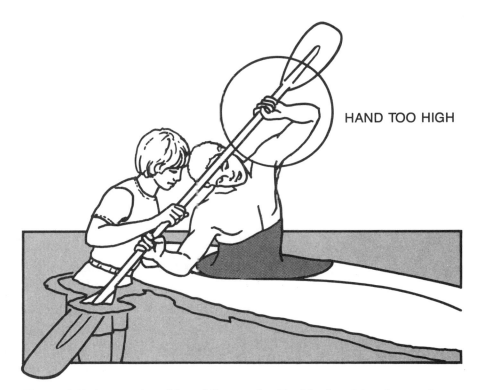

HAND TOO HIGH

Figure 6.7: An overhead hand "unmasked" with the aide of an assistant.

commit your roll technique to memory and everlasting habit, check to be sure it isn't subtly booby-trapped.

Critique your paddle blade control by having your assistant freeze the positions of your paddle shaft and kayak just as you complete your roll. Your assistant places one hand on the kayak's stern and one hand on the paddle shaft, as shown in figure 6.7. An inboard hand or arm that has drifted above your forehead gives poor purchase and causes the paddle to dive. If both hands are held a foot or more in front of your chest, you create a mechanically weak link between the paddle and your trunk. An inboard hand pushed forward or an outboard hand pulled back (as if in a forward stroke), generates a turning rather than a rolling motion, and makes your roll much less reliable. Energy that goes into moving the boat forward or turning it is wasted. It does not help you rotate the kayak upright.

The Advanced Brace Roll

I regard learning the basic brace roll as a step toward learning the advanced brace roll. Those who have difficulty holding the paddle in the air during the basic brace roll often learn the advanced brace roll by accident. The most obvious difference between the two rolls is that the paddle is pulled through the water during the sweep stroke of the advanced brace roll—a small difference with big advantages.

There is no attempt to hipsnap the kayak during the sweep stroke of either brace roll. Because there is no hipsnap during the sweep stroke, there is no downward pressure on the paddle either. This means that if the paddle has a climbing blade angle it will plane vigorously upward when pulled sideways through the water, just like it does in the sweep roll. This is a significant benefit that you sacrifice with an "air sweep." Since you position the blade away from the boat anyway, moving the paddle through the water serves to hold the paddle and the paddler on the surface.

Those of you without the flexibility to hold your paddle on the surface with the boat flat in the water will find this through-the-water sweep helps you complete the sweep stroke in a less extreme side-leaning posture. The kayak may rotate as much as 20 or 30 degrees by the time the paddle reaches brace position, without any sort of hipsnap (see figures 6.8 a and b). This makes the advanced brace roll feel more natural and comfortable than the basic technique.

The advantage cited most often for using a through-the-water sweep is that it significantly increases the reliability of your roll when

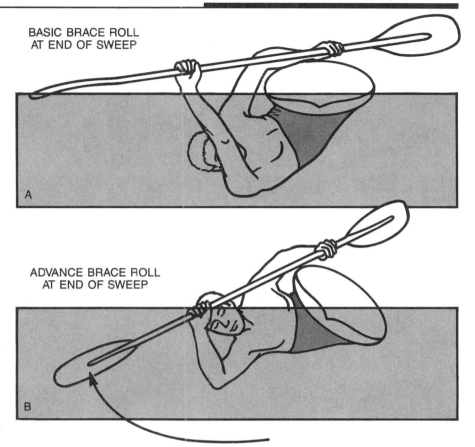

BASIC BRACE ROLL
AT END OF SWEEP

A

ADVANCE BRACE ROLL
AT END OF SWEEP

B

*Figure 6.8 a,b: A This kayak lies flat in the water at the end of a basic brace roll sweep stroke. The lack of boat motion prevents your head from reaching the surface and requires a strained body posture to hold the outboard blade in the air. B In contrast, the advanced brace roll sweep stroke **will** rotate the kayak, which allows your head to reach the surface without an extreme torso lean.*

working against a river current, in other words, a roll on the upstream side of the kayak. A basic brace roll on the upstream side of the boat may allow the current to push the upstream rail, the outboard blade, and the paddler's body further underwater before the paddle is in position to permit a hipsnap. This is most likely to occur if the outboard blade is underwater at the start of the roll, and will markedly reduce your chances for success (see figure 6.9). An advanced brace roll, however, will allow you to slice your blade upward during the sweep stroke, and rotate both you and the kayak toward the surface, even on the upstream side of the boat.

The effectiveness of the advanced brace roll depends on good timing. The sweep stroke must be done moderately fast to plane upward and offer enough purchase to keep the paddle and paddler near the surface. When the outboard blade reaches a position perpendicular to the kayak, the sweep must be followed immediately by the hipsnap, or the

▪ The effectiveness of the advanced brace roll depends on good timing.

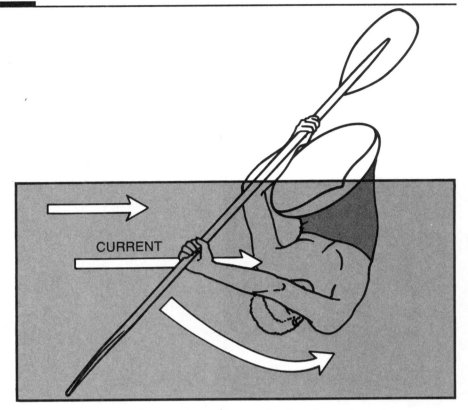

Figure 6.9: Current flowing rapidly past the kayak can impair an upstream basic brace roll. This won't occur if the kayak is moving downstream at the same speed as the current.

paddle and paddler will settle back into the water. The hipsnap follows the sweep without pause; treat it as if it were the end phase of the sweep stroke.

So Which Roll Is For You?

There are fanatical proponents (who are also excellent kayakers!) of each of the three roll techniques I've described: the basic brace roll, the advanced brace roll, and the sweep roll. All three follow the guidelines outlined in chapter 4 for a reliable, effective roll.

My opinions about the Eskimo roll, anyone's opinions, are shaped by personal experience. The first roll I learned was a basic brace roll, which evolved into an advanced brace roll. I use the advanced brace roll for my right-hand paddle roll, but my left-hand roll is a sweep roll. Perhaps it evolved that way because the wrist position on completion of a left-hand roll is in extension (cocked backward), which I can maintain easier with a back-leaning sweep roll. Also, my inboard arm kept hitting my kayak's rail during left-hand rolls, and this didn't happen when I began to sweep my blade well away from the boat and started hip rotation early.

I resort to the basic brace roll on the rare occasion that I miss my first several roll attempts. It was the first roll I learned, and there is at least one good reason to use it when necessary: good timing is not required. I've noticed that tired paddlers tend to lean on their paddles more, and hipsnap less. This grave disruption in sweep/hipsnap timing almost always causes the paddle to dive in highly aerated water (which offers the paddle little support). The basic brace roll forces you to push the outboard blade to the surface instead of leaning on it, and does not require timing the hipsnap to the sweep stroke.

I vividly remember two occasions when the basic brace roll saved my day: once after accidentally running two large, paired waterfalls, and again in an eddy line below a large drop. In each case the water was chaotic, I was tired, and low on air. In each case, after failing to roll upright on several tries, my final successful attempt was a basic brace roll. I pushed the paddle up onto the surface away from the kayak, and then just whaled on the hipsnap without concern for a climbing blade angle or sweep-hipsnap timing.

I can truly say that I like and use all three of these rolls. The sweep roll and the advanced brace roll are exceptionally good, while the basic brace roll is only slightly less reliable on the river. However, if any of these rolls fail on the upstream side of the kayak, they almost always succeed if the first roll is immediately followed by a second roll on the opposite side (the "off-side" paddle roll is fully discussed in the next chapter).

Which roll should you use? I suggest you initially learn which ever of these three rolls is closest to the one used by the person or persons you paddle with and who will help teach you to roll. If you choose the sweep roll, the left-handed roll may be somewhat easier to learn than the right. After gaining confidence with one roll (which may take a year or more!), experiment, and learn the others.

Each of these three rolls teaches you something a little different about blade control, edge control, lean, and balance. For instance, a basic brace roll teaches you how to bring your head and hands to the surface without using your paddle. During a hands roll (to be discussed in chapter 10) your head and hands move toward the surface in precisely this manner. Learning several different Eskimo rolls is not an insurmountable task, and it gives you something to do when you're not running rapids. A frame by frame comparison of the advanced brace roll and the sweep roll, in figure 6.10, shows that their similarities far outnumber their differences.

You're going to use the roll you feel most comfortable with, and it won't hurt to mix and match these three techniques. Few paddlers have rolls that are purely sweep or purely brace anyway. Without trying, most paddlers develop a synthesis of brace and sweep roll technique, making

▪ After gaining confidence with one roll, experiment, and learn the others.

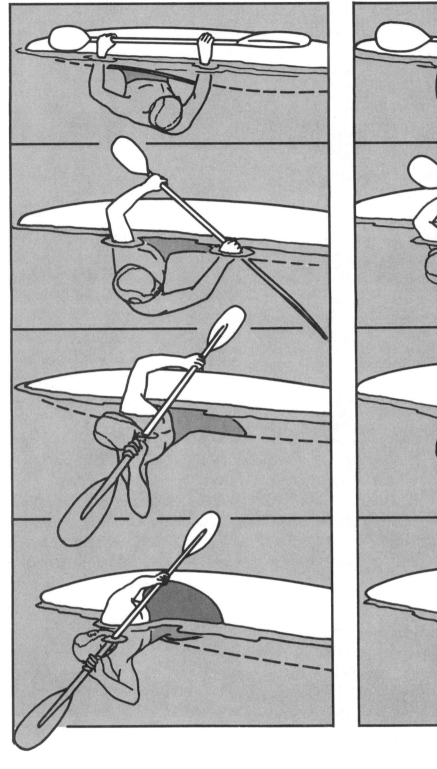
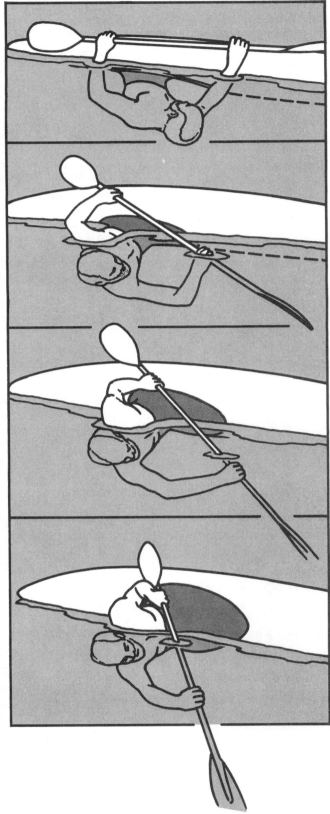

Figure 6.10 a-d: A comparison of the advanced brace roll (on the left) and the sweep roll in about 45 degree increments of boat rotation. The similarities are extensive. Body lean is nearly identical for a given degree of boat rotation. The paddle remains near the surface throughout both rolls.

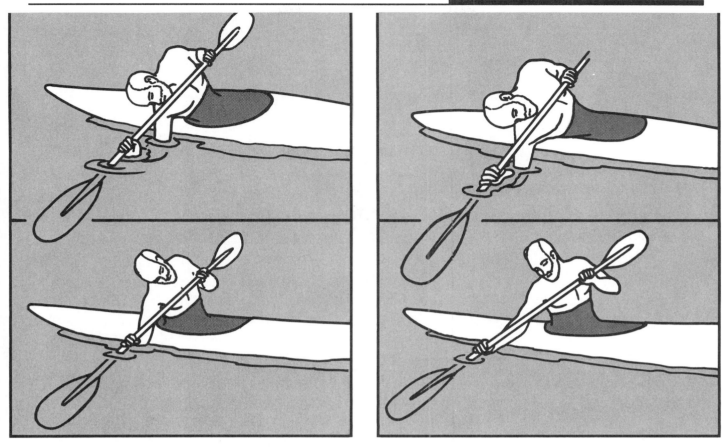

Figure 6.10 e,f: Comparison of advanced brace roll (on left) and the sweep roll. Good hip rotation coupled with near-the-surface outboard blades in both rolls results in a blending of hipsnap and recovery into one motion.

them hard to tell apart. Sweep rollers may end with a small brace stroke, or may allow the anchor hand to pass over the hull as in a brace roll. Brace rollers may roll up mostly during the preliminary sweep stroke by adding in a little early hip rotation. There is no one best roll technique for everyone. In the end, the technique that you find works best for you will undoubtedly be unique to your physique and temperament.

There are two possible directions in which to roll a kayak: a setup on your left side lets you sweep your right blade (a right-hand roll), whereas a setup on your right side lets you sweep your left blade (a left-hand roll). I think it safe to say that beginners learn only one of these. Which is your "off-side"? It is the side you don't roll well on, which is usually the side you didn't learn first. In some West Coast kayak schools, paddlers first learn a left-hand roll (which seems to complement the sweep roll), although it is probably more common to learn a right-hand roll first. Since my initial descriptions were of right-hand rolls, here we'll focus on left-hand rolls.

There are many reasons to acquire an off-side roll. If your on-side roll fails, you'll often find your paddle in position to execute a roll on the off-side. Without an off-side roll the paddle must be moved underwater from one side of the boat to the other, back into the on-side setup position. This takes effort, decreases your air reserves, and increases the chances of your body striking an underwater rock. If you initially find yourself in the off-side setup position, it is likewise fastest and safest to roll upright without changing sides. Another consideration is that a kayak may be held in a hydraulic or against a rock in such a way that rolling upright is only possible on your off-side.

The off-side roll is not just unfamiliar to the novice from lack of use, it feels, and is, different from its on-side counterpart. The reason for this difference lies in the use of 90 degree offset paddle blades, which are offset to cut down on wind resistance. If a right hand control paddle is held securely in the right power grip position (as it would be for a right forward stroke), the off-side roll will require a wrist position nearly 90 degrees different from the on-side roll. If your paddle blades are not offset (a rarity nowadays), right and left hand rolls become mirror images of each other, and feel nearly the same.

The wrist position (flexed, straight, or extended) used during any roll can be practiced sitting in your kayak on dry land, as described in chapter 5. Hold the paddle shaft firmly in a right power grip position, without loosening or repositioning your grip. Lean forward into your off-side setup position holding the paddle so your outboard blade has a climbing blade angle. Then, sit up and move the outboard blade to the opposite side of the boat, and hold the shaft so the end of your blade rests flat on the floor, the position it would be in at roll completion. During the actual roll your wrists change position just as they do here. Compare the on-side and off-side wrist positions and how they change during the mid-portion of the roll.

■ A kayak may be held in a hydraulic or against a rock in such a way that rolling upright is only possible on your off-side.

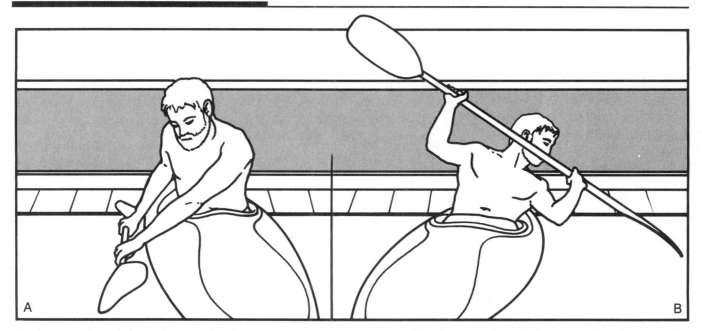

Figure 7.1 a,b: While sitting on the floor, move your wrists smoothly through their full range of motion; a left-handed roll—from setup to roll completion.

You should find that your wrists are initially strongly cocked (flexed) for a right-hand roll (leaning toward the left deck), and straightened to the neutral position at roll completion. During the setup for a left-hand roll (leaning toward the right deck), the wrists are initially held straight, and then fully extended at roll completion, as shown in figure 7.1. You'll find yourself leaning backward at the completion of a left-hand roll, with your forearms raised much higher than its right-hand counterpart. The extended wrist, raised forearm, and increased back lean account for the different feeling of the left-hand roll.

You can minimize the back lean during a left-hand roll by loosening your left hand's grip on the paddle, allowing the shaft to spin slightly, as in figure 7.2. Do not loosen the firm right-hand grip on your right-hand control paddle, so blade control is maintained. Using the wrist position exercise for a left-hand roll, experiment with loosening your grip with the outboard hand and see what effect it has on your final body position. This is a useful option; it isn't essential to the roll.

There are alternate methods of doing the left-hand paddle roll, but I don't recommend any of them. For instance, you could regrip the paddle shaft in a left power grip position (as you would for a left forward stroke). The change in grip allows you to do your left-hand roll the same way you do a right-hand roll, with flexed wrists in the setup position that move into a neutral wrist position during the hipsnap; but flipping in a kayak is usually unexpected, and you don't have a chance to think about which side you'll have to roll on. Learning different paddle grips for particular rolls adds an element of complexity you don't need.

■ Learning different paddle grips for particular rolls adds an element of complexity you don't need.

Figure 7.2: Loosening the grip on the outboard paddle shaft and letting it spin in your hand during a left-handed roll will allow you to complete the roll with much less back lean.

A left-hand roll using a right-hand power grip is simple and fast, and requires no last second corrections in grip. As the difficulty and danger of the rivers you paddle increase, it becomes essential to master your off-side roll. Practice your off-side roll frequently on flat water, and when the occasion arises, on the river. With experience and lots and lots of rolls, one day you'll roll up after playing in a wave or hydraulic and won't recall which side you came up on! At that moment you no longer use an on-side or an off-side roll. The roll has become instinctive, something you simply do.

8 · The Diving Paddle, Cause and Cure

■ A good roll can be distinguished from a bad roll by the position of the paddle immediately after the hipsnap and recovery.

Most paddlers who learn to roll under close supervision are amazed at how easy it is to roll upright the first time they do it on their own. Congratulations are certainly in order for that first unassisted roll. You are, however, embarking upon a period during which your ability to roll will come and go. Some days your roll will feel effortless, and other days you will feel you are working hard to come upright.

Even after thoroughly learning a roll, you can expect to go through a brief period during which that roll's timing or coordination is upset as you learn a different roll, or an off-side roll. You will constantly want to fine-tune your "good" rolls and troubleshoot those that are not yet running smoothly. This chapter offers some suggestions to help you recognize roll techniques that are not yet up to snuff, and to help you fix them. It will be especially useful to the people whose roll seems to work well enough on flat water, but inexplicably fails them on the river.

A good roll can be distinguished from a bad roll by the position of the paddle immediately after the hipsnap and recovery. Throughout a well-executed roll the outboard paddle blade will remain near the surface, leaving more than 90 degrees of vertical paddle motion for bracing at roll completion. I call this a 100% margin of safety; if a brace is needed, it's available. If the roll is not successfully completed by the end of the hipsnap, an attempt is usually made to salvage the roll by pulling down on the paddle, which causes it to dive. The paddle shaft becomes more vertical, and the anchor hand rises with the shaft to a position overhead or on the same side of the boat as the outboard hand (look again at figure 3.3 c, which shows this phenomenon). The deeply submerged paddle offers no margin of safety. Drifting across even a small eddy line with the paddle in this position can tip the kayak over because balance is marginal, and no brace is available.

A vertical paddle, however, is only a symptom of a poor roll; it does not tell you which part of the roll is at fault. Curing a sick roll depends on identifying the cause of the problem. My approach to troubleshooting a sick roll is to regard the sweep stroke as functionally independent of the hipsnap. An effective setup and sweep keeps the paddle near the surface of the water throughout the sweep, regardless of the type of roll employed. If the paddle is not near the surface at the end of the sweep, the setup and sweep are not working well. If the sweep stroke succeeds in bringing the paddle to the surface and the roll fails, either the hipsnap or the recovery is not working well.

It is sometimes hard to tell whether your blade approaches the surface during the sweep, because it often remains underwater and is in motion throughout the roll. The "sweep test" described below will tell you whether or not your blade stays near the surface. If your sweep stroke fails the test, Section 1 of this chapter should help you identify at least part of the problem. If your sweep stroke passes the test, roll problems are more likely to involve the hipsnap or recovery, and these are addressed in Section 2. There is some redundancy between Sections 1 and 2 because the sweep and hipsnap overlap during most rolls.

These common errors and my solutions to them are far from being an all-inclusive listing. There are many, many ways to do a roll poorly, and almost everyone has their pet remedies. In this chapter, I hope to get you thinking in some logical way about what you actually do during your roll. With luck, you'll recognize the very thing that has your roll booby-trapped, and be able to change your technique accordingly. You'll find this chapter to be a good review of all the important concepts presented in the first half of the book.

Sweep Test: To determine the effectiveness of your sweep, have two friends suspend a long pole (like those used to clean pools) 12 inches under the water's surface and parallel to your kayak. Sweeping your blade above the pole during your roll is the objective. Have each assistant hold one end of the kayak in one hand and the pole in the other in order to keep the pole a fixed distance from your boat. This distance is about one half to two thirds the length of your paddle, not so close that the paddle can pass over the pole and then downward, but not so far away that your outboard blade won't reach it with a normal sweep stroke. This arrangement is shown in figure 8.1.

Turn upside down and roll back upright. It may help to wear a SCUBA mask so that you can watch your paddle. If you succeed in sweeping above the pole while wearing a mask, you can do so without one, and with your eyes shut. Try to hold your outboard blade several inches above the surface during the sweep of a basic brace roll. Any roll attempt where the paddle passes below the pole should be considered to have failed the test.

There are many technical reasons you might have trouble sweeping your paddle blade across the surface. A less tangible reason is that it takes time and experience for most people to learn where "up" is when they are upside down in a kayak. All rolls become easier when you are able to lean up to the surface and reach up toward the surface during the sweep, much as you would reach up for an object on the upper shelf of the kitchen cupboard. The sweep test, therefore, does more for you than just grade your sweep, it can be an active aid to learning "up".

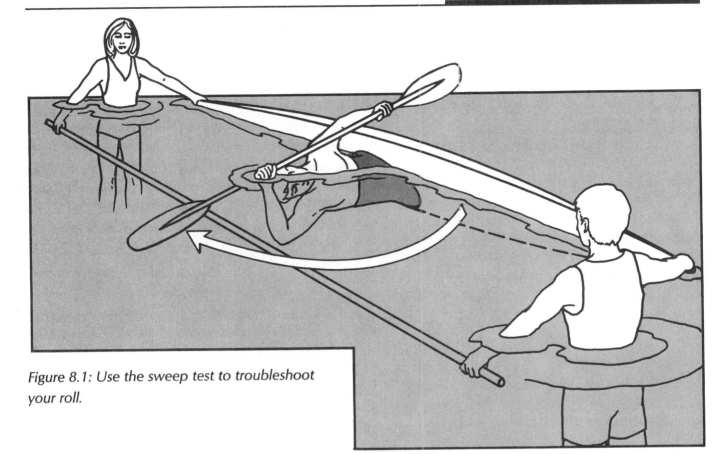

Figure 8.1: Use the sweep test to troubleshoot your roll.

Section 1. Causes of a Diving Paddle Due to the Setup or Sweep

A. Problem: The setup position is not attained before the sweep is started.

Many beginning and intermediate paddlers think they set up before the sweep, but do not. In their anxiousness to roll upright, they begin to sweep the paddle before it is parallel to either the water's surface or the boat. With one or both hands away from the boat's side, they lose any sense of where the paddle is, and usually end up sweeping the blade downward, and not across the surface. The solution is to set up early with both wrists against the boat's rail before the kayak tips all the way over. The sweep can then begin the moment the boat rolls fully upside down.

A related problem occurs when the kayak doesn't roll fully upside down. An affliction of beginners (to which more experienced paddlers become immunized) is to fall into the water sitting upright, as in figure 8.2 a, instead of in the tucked forward setup position. The flotation jacket then acts like a high brace stroke to stop or slow the boat's rotation. Most of the momentum which would have helped carry you under the boat is lost, leaving the paddle deeply submerged and the boat on edge (figure 8.2 b). Avoid this entire problem by quickly leaning forward into the setup position when you flip, before your body enters the water.

If you do get "stuck" under the boat (and this is not infrequent when a small person wears a high flotation jacket), finish leaning all the way forward, nose to deck and forearms against the side of the boat. This will often move your flotation jacket to the side of the kayak you are trying to roll up on, and allow the paddle to float to the surface. If it does not, taking a quick underwater draw stroke or rocking your hips will often succeed. As a last resort, it may become necessary to slide the paddle between your chest and the kayak's deck in order to set up on the opposite side of the boat.

B. Problem: The sweep stroke stops before 90° or extends well past 90° before the hipsnap is initiated (Brace roll).

Feel where "perpendicular to the boat" is in space, as your assistant guides you, with your eyes shut, into the correct position for the hipsnap. Your spacial orientation will be aided by starting from the same setup position each time. If your sweep stops before or after the perpendicular, the blade will give poor purchase and sink, and your ability to hipsnap may be impaired.

C. Problem: You hold your paddle blade in a negative angle of attack during the setup and sweep.

A blade that starts with a positive (climbing) angle will usually remain on the surface throughout the sweep, whereas a negative blade angle will cause the blade to dive steeply. Beginners often err in this way because they hold the paddle shaft loosely in their anchor hand when leaning forward into the setup position, or they don't cock

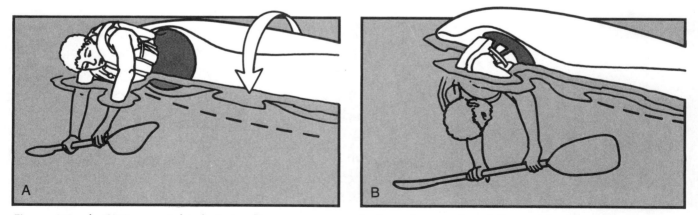

Figure 8.2 a,b: Sitting upright during a flip may prevent the boat from rolling fully upside down.

their wrists enough to angle the blade correctly. The anchor hand should be held with a firm, closed grip. Cocking or extending your wrists fully with a closed grip may take some practice, but it's the only way you'll be able to control your blade angle.

D. Problem: The roll starts from a good setup position but the blade is unconsciously pulled downward instead of being swept out to the side.

This is a very common error. Many paddlers forget to sweep and instead pull downward on the paddle as if trying to roll the boat using a forward stroke. They'll also instinctively pull down on the paddle if it begins to rapidly sink because of poor purchase. During the sweep roll this occurs when the blade is held at too large an angle of attack (so the blade "stalls" and sinks), or hip rotation is begun before the sweep stroke becomes effective.

In each instance, the paddle blade sinks underwater near the bow of the boat and is pulled, still deeply submerged, toward the stern. Unfortunately, the not-yet-righted kayak will move forward while the paddler trails behind leaning on a vertical paddle for support.

The solution to this problem is to keep the blade in a slight to moderate climbing angle relative to the water's surface, initially move it smoothly *away* from the boat across the water's surface with a backhand motion, and begin to rotate the kayak upright only after the blade begins to offer purchase. This proper use of your paddle will help rotate the kayak and move it *under* you, not away from you.

E. Problem: Power punching

Some paddlers deliberately punch the anchor hand skyward in order to drive the paddle forcefully downward as their means of obtaining paddle support. This roll feels powerful because so much unnecessary energy is expended. It may look effective on flat water, but it is an undependable whitewater roll with a small margin for error. The anchor hand and arm are invariably raised to head level or higher in mid-roll, creating the nefarious vertical paddle. As the paddle dives, it becomes less effective in rotating the boat, and predictably decreases the safety margin to zero. Abandon this technique and learn a better, more reliable one.

If power punching represented a philosophical attitude about rolling, then the message I have tried to put across in this book is diametrically opposed to it. I suggest you decrease the pressure on your paddle by concentrating on driving with the knees, hip rotation, and a strong reversal in body lean. The power puncher assumes the opposite position by maximizing pressure on the paddle, and therefore increasing his dependence on it.

F. Problem: Premature lifting of the head out of the water.

This is the single greatest enemy of an effective roll, and can occur both during and after the sweep. The problem is universal, and occurs because your head should come out of the water after the kayak is rolled upright—a "wait" that conflicts with deeply rooted instincts to breathe NOW. Giving in to instinct may result in one breath now, but it will not help you roll the kayak upright so you can breath afterward.

Lifting your head prematurely vastly increases the pressure on your paddle, which rapidly sinks deeper. In order to raise your head upward, you will unconsciously use your upper knee for support, which stops the reversal of body lean necessary for completion of the hipsnap and kills the boat's rolling momentum.

Your chest, arms, and float jacket contribute to the support platform offered by the paddle. It would be ludicrous to lift the paddle out of the water before the completion of the roll is assured; it is equally harmful to lift your head or trunk out of the water too early. Allow your body and head to remain in the water during the sweep, and keep your head low throughout the hipsnap by looking downward at the water or watching your paddle blade.

Section 2. Causes of a Diving Paddle that Occur After the Sweep

A. Problem: Premature lifting of the head out of the water.

This is the most frequent problem that occurs after the sweep, and is discussed in Section 1 F. A premature head lift is most obvious when it is done instead of doing the hipsnap, but subtle or obvious, it is a big negative factor when it occurs during any roll.

B. Problem: A late hipsnap (Advanced Brace roll).

Beginners often have a tendency to pause between the sweep and the hipsnap, which allows the paddle to sink unnecessarily. This undoubtedly occurs because each part of the brace roll is taught in sequence: first the sweep, and then the hipsnap. It is important to realize that paddle movement during the sweep and hipsnap is one fluid motion (changing from a horizontal to a passive vertical movement); begin the hipsnap the moment the blade reaches a position 90° from the boat. There should be no pause or hesitation.

C. Problem: A slow or inadequate hipsnap (Brace roll).

Like a late hipsnap, a slow hipsnap gives the paddle time to sink so that paddle purchase is lost before the kayak can fully rotate underneath you. A good sweep does little to compensate for a poor hipsnap, but a good hipsnap easily compensates for a poor sweep and poor purchase. Only momentary paddle purchase is needed if you do the hipsnap smoothly and confidently.

Don't make the mistake of trying to strengthen your hipsnap by pulling more forcefully down on the paddle. Instead, start the hipsnap with a brisk movement of your knee toward the paddle. When boat rotation is initiated through knee pressure, all your energy is concentrated in turning the boat about its axis, and little is wasted on lifting your head or trunk. Once the hipsnap is begun, maintain knee pressure until the kayak has rolled completely upright and balance is restored.

D. Problem: Slow or inadequate hip rotation (Sweep roll).

During the sweep roll, the boat must be rotated 180° while your paddle, head, and trunk move across the water's surface during the sweep. Think of initiating rotation with knee pressure when the sweep starts away from the boat. There should actually be a split-second delay in hip rotation that allows the paddle to begin its movement across the surface and develop purchase on the water, but this is a fine point. The more common problem is not to initiate hip rotation early enough. The kayak should be rotated almost fully upright by the time the sweep reaches 90°; if it is not, earlier or more deliberate knee pressure is needed.

E. Problem: Completing the roll with straight elbows and an overhead paddle (Brace roll).

The anchor hand is most effective when held close to your chest; This position allows the outboard paddle blade to move in an arc around the long axis of the kayak, much like the blades of a riverboat paddle-wheel move around its axle. Before the hipsnap, the kayak's hull rests between your arm and chest. You must consciously bend your elbow and pull your anchor hand to your chest in mid-hipsnap when the kayak's hull has rotated out of your way. This is not a natural movement for most beginners. If the elbow remains straight throughout the hipsnap, it will usually force the anchor hand into an overhead position, and the entire paddle becomes less effective (in the same way an overhead brace is less effective than a high brace).

F. Problem: A forward stroke during the hipsnap (Brace roll).

It is not uncommon for brace rollers to convert the high brace stroke into a forward/turning stroke during the hipsnap. This will decrease rotation forces, and cause the boat to turn and move forward instead. The recovery may become strained, and you may find yourself leaning on a diving paddle before the roll is completed.

You can practice keeping your hands (and, therefore, the paddle) perpendicular to the kayak's axis of rotation by using the exercise shown in figure 6.6, or by resting your outboard blade on the side of a pool at water level and doing several hipsnaps. Your boat should remain nearly parallel to the side of the pool, and not move forward. As a final test, position yourself about six to eight feet from the side of the pool, and see if you can roll your kayak while keeping it parallel to the pool's edge, from roll beginning to end. (A sweep roll will cause some forward turning motion even if it is done well.)

I've focused on the paddle roll because a reliable roll, one you have confidence in, is central to your learning more advanced skills. It is also the key to having a joyful, unintimidating, river experience. Practice each roll you know in the pool and on flat sections of a river until rolling your kayak is like breathing or walking. When you lose all apprehension over flipping in safe water, you'll be able to focus your energies fully on learning new techniques, and on fine-tuning your boat control skills.

9 · Advanced Bracing

It is not necessary to master each technique I present to be able to play on whitewater. However, the more control you have over your boat on flat water, the more confidence you'll gain and the faster you'll progress on whitewater. Boat control is the name of this game; challenge yourself!

Extreme High Brace Positions

The high brace can be executed with increasingly greater edge tilts until the kayak is literally upside down. It's not possible to keep your head over the deck in an extreme edge tilt, so when the kayak no longer offers support, it is probably best to allow the water to cushion your fall before hipsnapping the kayak upright. Hold your blade as near the surface as possible as you roll into the water, and when you feel the momentary support the water offers, hipsnap the boat upright, as in 9.1 a through c. Then, and only then, allow your head to move out of the water and over the boat.

Experiment with extreme high brace positions on both sides, but keep a few precautions in mind:

• If the boat should turn all the way over, don't fall on an outstretched arm. Keep your outboard elbow and shoulder flexed slightly to cushion your fall into the water. If your arm is raised as your paddle impacts the water, you may stretch the muscles under your arm or injure your shoulder (figure 9.2).

• Be sure to lower your inboard hand during the hipsnap; it increases the effectiveness of your paddle and protects your shoulder. Another advantage of this is that your outboard blade will tend to plane upward as it approaches the kayak. This is only slightly exaggerated in the figure 9.1 series, where the outboard blade rises during the brace even though it is being used to support the hipsnap.

• On whitewater, discretion is the better part of valor, meaning it is usually more appropriate to tuck into the setup position and roll the kayak than to try to salvage a near flip with an extreme high brace. There are no demerits given for rolling your kayak. An extreme high brace isn't any faster than a roll, and it is more likely to cause injury by stressing your shoulder. Don't do that. If you are about to flip over, just tuck and roll.

▪ An extreme high brace isn't any faster than a roll, and it is more likely to cause injury by stressing your shoulder.

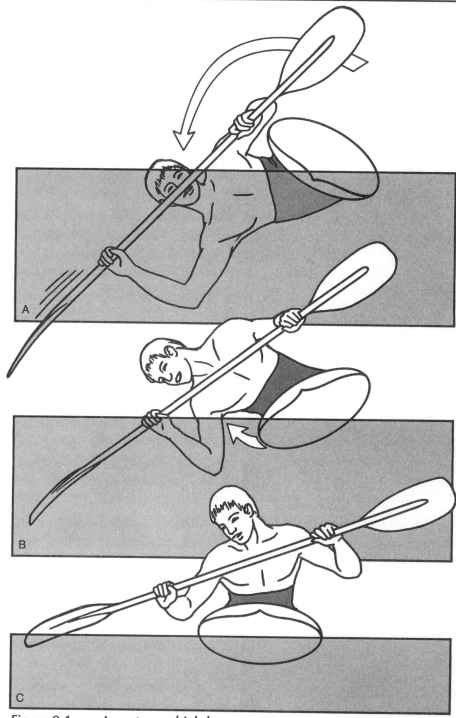

Figure 9.1 a-c: An extreme high brace.

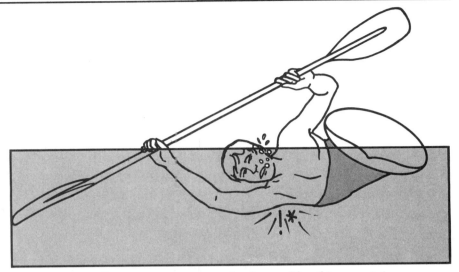

Figure 9.2: "Falling" on an outstretched arm, like this, can injure your arm or shoulder.

Sculling Brace Strokes

Continuous brace strokes, which I call a sustained brace, are sometimes needed to keep the kayak upright when side-surfing. Sculling is one such technique. Hold the paddle as for a high brace stroke, and move your blade back and forth in a figure-of-eight pattern, using only the power face of the blade to obtain purchase, as shown in figure 9.3. Each time the power face of the blade slices from side to side, plane it upward to the surface so the purchase it offers on the water is self-renewing.

Sculling requires a lot of forearm and wrist motion if your paddle is gripped firmly in both hands. Both wrists fully flex and then extend with each back and forth motion. It is less fatiguing to control these constant changes in blade angle by keeping a firm grip with your anchor hand, and allowing the shaft to spin slightly in a loosened outboard hand. While the anchor hand is held close to the body and controls blade angle, its outboard counterpart supplies power to the sculling blade, though most paddlers probably aren't aware of which wrist they use for what. Sculling practice is an excellent way to improve blade control on flat water.

Since you use only the power face of the blade when sculling, each backstroke requires fully extended wrists and causes a momentary back/side lean toward the water to give the blade a climbing angle. The upper body posture that results is a lean into the water and away from the boat, committing you to the scull for support. Practice increasing your lean into the water until you get your face wet on either side of the boat. Keep the sculling blade as close to the surface as possible. A high brace/hipsnap easily rights the kayak.

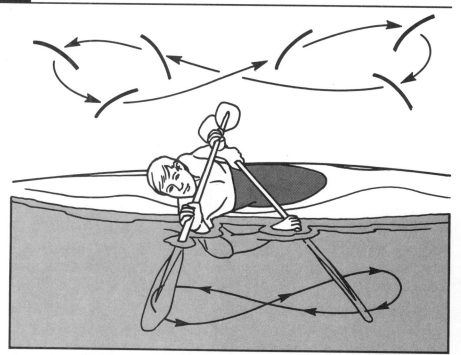

Figure 9.3: The "back stroke" of a sculling brace requires a back lean because only the power face of the blade is used.

A Sculling Draw Stroke

Do a sculling draw stroke in the same way as a sculling brace stroke, but hold the blade vertically instead of horizontally. That acts to pull the boat sideways in the water (figure 9.4). This sustained draw stroke is not used to support your weight, so keep your weight over the kayak and don't lean on the blade. You can try a sculling draw stroke at the bow of the boat to move the kayak in a slow forward turn.

A Sculling Draw/Brace Stroke

Commit yourself to the sculling brace stroke for support, while moving the kayak sideways by adding a sculling draw component. If the paddle shaft becomes too vertical or your scull isn't fast enough, you'll tip all the way over and end up hanging from the upside down kayak. Don't let that stop you; by leaning up toward the surface you can continue to scull the boat sideways even though your head is under water.

Work your way up to sculling fifteen feet sideways, hipsnap upright, and scull your way back in the other direction. Remember to scull your outboard blade all the way up to the surface before you do the hipsnap!

Figure 9.4: A sculling draw stroke moves the kayak sideways, toward the sculling blade.

A Sustained Brace Using Sweep Strokes

Alternating forward and back sweep strokes is an excellent way to achieve a sustained brace. Start with the boat flat in the water in order to learn how to link each forward and back sweep smoothly. Use only the back face of the paddle blade on the back sweep. Keep the movement continuous and the blade flat by using the inboard hand to control the rapid flip of the blade as it reaches the end of each arc, while the outboard hand grips the paddle loosely to permit rapid shaft rotation. Controlling your blade angle with the outboard hand requires larger arm movements and increases fatigue.

Next, tilt the boat on its edge and hold it there by lifting your knee and leaning as far in toward the boat as you can. The idea is to keep most of your weight over the boat while using the sweep strokes primarily for balance, as shown in figure 9.5. Leaning away from the boat will markedly increase the weight on your paddle, and you'll have to work much harder to stay upright. The tighter your inward lean, the steeper you can hold the kayak on edge. Increase your edge tilt until you can barely stay upright using linked sweep strokes, and then work up to holding this position for

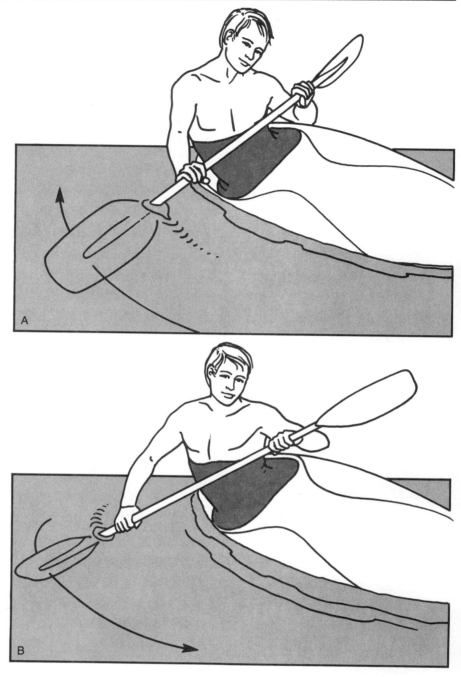

THE BACK SWEEP USES THE BACK SIDE
OF THE PADDLE BLADE.

THE FORWARD SWEEP USES THE
BLADE'S POWER FACE.

Figure 9.5 a,b: Linked sweep strokes are stronger than a scull and allow you to sit upright. This is because the back face of the blade is used during the back stroke.

a minute or longer. This is an excellent practice drill which closely duplicates side-surfing extreme whitewater.

Chris Spelius, a whitewater instructor at the Nantahala Outdoor Center in North Carolina, taught me this technique and calls it "bread-and-buttering" with your paddle blade. Besides teaching an effective forward and back sweep stroke, it develops strength in the pelvis and trunk that will help you sit upright while holding your boat on edge, a skill essential to river playing. It is more complex than a sculling motion, but frequently more useful in playboating situations. We'll compare these two techniques further in chapter 15, which covers "Hole Playing." Practice a bread-and-butter stroke often and don't forget to give your off-side equal attention.

Other Flatwater Practice Maneuvers

Flat water practice allows you to approach a state of complete familiarity with your kayak, and increases your ability to remain oriented when your body is underwater. This won't happen overnight, and it won't necessarily happen in your first two or three years of paddling; but it's an attainable goal. Don't hesitate to combine the skills you've learned up to this point. Here are a few maneuvers to strive toward and conquer:

1. Alternate rolling to your left and right sides, using each roll you know.
2. Roll upside down holding the paddle in your right hand; pass the paddle across the top of the boat to your left hand, setup on your left side, regrip your paddle, and roll upright. Repeat this, passing the paddle in the other direction.
3. Roll upside down into the setup position; then slide the paddle between your chest and the kayak's deck into the setup position on the opposite side, and roll upright. Repeat this until you can pass the paddle smoothly and roll in both directions.
4. Roll upside down, setup, and roll to a boat position 45° to 60° less than fully upright. Sustain this boat tilt for ten seconds by using sculling or sweep strokes. Quickly tuck into the setup position allowing your body to fall back into the water. Setup and again hipsnap to a boat position 45° to 60° less than fully upright on the opposite side. Sustain this edge tilt with a sculling or sweep brace for ten seconds before completing your roll. A sculling stroke will keep your body in or close to the water during this maneuver; a sustained sweep brace will keep your body well out of the water. Practice both.

This exercise teaches you paddle blade and boat control, and it also gives some insight into what you can do to salvage an almost completed roll on whitewater. Initiating a strong back sweep brace when it looks like your roll is about to fail, followed by several brisk bread-and-butter strokes, will usually help you regain control of your edges and roll upright.

5.   Scull/draw ten feet to one side and then, allowing your body and paddle to sink under the boat, move to the opposite side and scull/draw ten feet the other way. High brace upright and then repeat the exercise in the other direction.

These flat water acrobatics will be disorienting at first. When your head is underwater and you're trying to scull sideways, it's often difficult to keep in mind where "up" is. It's easy to lean backward and under the kayak instead of maintaining a strong lean away from the boat and up toward the surface. One of the main goals in playing these games is to become oriented to all parts of your boat and the surface when upside down. This ability to remain oriented pays big dividends in whitewater, and makes learning a hands roll much, much easier.

Why learn a hands roll? One good reason is that kayaking without a paddle is fun! There is an indescribable freedom in it, a joy, a charge. The best reasons, however, are that hands paddling quickly leads to improved boat control, dramatically increases your self-confidence, and a reliable hands roll will significantly improve your paddle roll. Many eddy turns, ferries, side and bow-surfs can be done in great part without reliance on a paddle; and, with one or both hands free, you'll find that paddle twirling becomes an exciting challenge. A reliable hands roll is nice to have when you're side-surfing a hole and miss catching your paddle after spinning it into the air . . .

There seem to be as many colors and flavors of hands roll as there are paddlers who do them. We're going to simplify the subject by dividing them into forward-leaning hands rolls (which can all be done with a side lean if desired), and hands rolls leaning to the back. All the basic principles regarding paddle rolls apply equally well to hands rolls. I describe a forward-leaning roll first, but I would initially learn a hands roll with a lean closest to that of your paddle roll. If you choose to learn a back-leaning hands roll, read this first section carefully anyway, because there is a great deal in common between all hands rolls, and this description is the most detailed.

Forward-Leaning Hands Rolls

A well-executed hands roll requires no more effort than a paddle roll, but hands rolls are unforgiving to errors of timing or technique because your hands have less surface area, and therefore provide less purchase on the

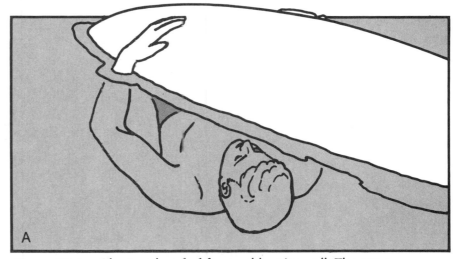

Figure 10.1 a: The two-handed forward leaning roll. The setup.

water. In my experience, the "two-handed" hands roll is the easiest one to learn and teach.

We'll call the hand that gives purchase and completes the roll the "support" hand. The other hand, which must be raised out of the water upon roll completion, we'll call the "assist" hand. All rolls are described as right handed, that is, completed with a right support hand. Left hand rolls are mirror images of right hand rolls, and are done in an identical manner.

The "Two-handed" Hands Roll

1. **Start Each Roll From the Same Setup Position**. The setup position for the hands roll is leaning forward with nose to deck and both hands against the boat's edges, as shown in figure 10.1 a. Like the setup for the paddle roll, this position protects your face and helps orient you to the surface. It takes only moments to become disoriented when underwater and out of the setup position. Newcomers to the hands roll often fail to set up, and may unknowingly initiate the hipsnap while leaning far back in the cockpit or with their head deeply underwater. Starting motionless from the setup position helps you develop the best sense of where your body is as you lean to the side and up toward the surface at the beginning of the roll.

2. **Move Your Head and Hands as Close as Possible to the Surface**. It is important to start the hipsnap with your head and hands near the surface, so that at the end of the hipsnap the kayak is fully

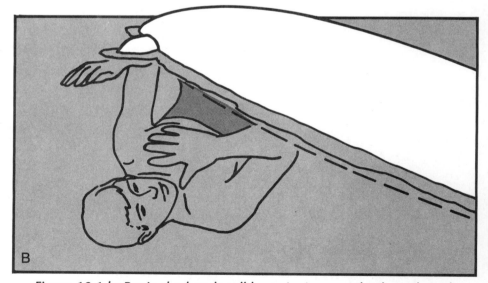

Figure 10.1 b: Begin the hands roll by swinging your body to the side and driving your head and hands toward the surface.

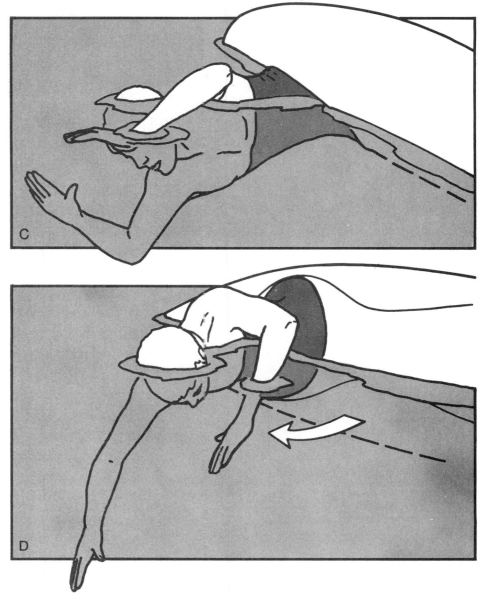

Figure 10.1 c,d: C *The purchase you get to support the hipsnap comes from extending your hands, arms, and trunk away from the boat.* D *Power the hipsnap with your torso, hips, and knees—not your hands.*

upright. Begin this movement toward the surface by leaning directly to the side toward your left hand and pulling your head upward using left knee pressure against the buoyant kayak for support. As you lean toward the surface, arch your back and turn your face and shoulders downward. Both palms should be open, with your right hand and forearm loosely paralleling your left, as in figure 10.1 b. Keeping your hands and arms uncrossed as you turn face downward avoids confusion.

    3. **Obtain Good "Hands Purchase" on the Water by Extending Your Trunk, Arms, and Hands Well Away From the Boat and Perpendicular to It**. Try to break the surface of the water with both hands as you extend your body as far from the boat as possible, as in figure

10.1 c. Your hands, arms, abdomen, chest, and flotation jacket all increase the surface area of the "platform" you will use to support your hipsnap. A slouched or tucked posture is useless. Your maximal lean to the left and toward the surface spring loads your body in preparation for the powerful hipsnap to the right.

4. **Powerfully Execute the Hipsnap as You Reach Full Hand and Arm Extension Away From the Boat**. The hipsnap occurs as you turn your hands downward and stretch away from the kayak. Initially, you depend on the kayak to help lift your body upward. As your hands and body move away from the boat and achieve purchase on the water, you transfer all the weight you were hanging from your left knee onto the support platform of your hands, arms, and chest. This unweights your left knee and allows you to execute a powerful hipsnap by driving with your right knee (figure 10.1 d).

There is no way to know by looking at a technically good roll that almost all the energy that goes into kayak rotation is generated by actively moving your right knee toward your right arm. This hipsnap motion occurs at your waist. The visible downward movement of the arms during a two-handed roll is mostly passive, a consequence of performing the hipsnap. Actively moving your arms toward your knee (plunging them down into the water) is a wasteful motion that occurs at the shoulders, and may interfere with the roll. This analogy may help you understand why. If you lie flat on the ground on your back, you can choose between raising your feet in the air (knees straight) toward your chest, or raising your chest in the air toward your feet. The two choices share muscle groups, but have completely different outcomes. For instance, it would be inconvenient to lift your feet in the air if you need to sit up to answer the phone. The same sort of thing occurs during the roll. Your choice is whether to rotate the deck of your boat toward your hands on the surface (rolling the kayak upright), or move your hands toward the upside-down kayak (pulling your body underwater). You must train your muscles so that you selectively pull your knee up to your extended hand, arm, and chest platform during the hipsnap. When the hipsnap is neglected in favor of pushing your hands downward, your hands become less effective, they sink deeper, and you'll be less likely to complete the roll.

5. **Use Head Tilt and Body Lean to Keep Your Head and Torso in the Water (Supported by It) Until the Kayak Rotates Under You, and Forces You Out of the Water**. At this point the kayak is rotating rapidly, and your objective is to minimize the amount of energy that it takes to move your body up and onto the boat. Any technique that avoids lifting the head out of the water during the hipsnap and does not interfere with boat rotation will accomplish this. Initially this roll should be completed with a strong forward lean, leaving your nose

■ Almost all the energy that goes into kayak rotation is generated by actively moving your right knee toward your right arm.

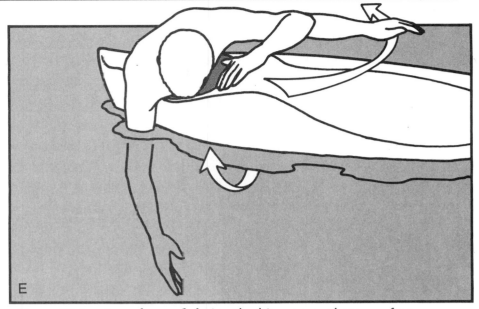

Figure 10.1 e: Lean forward during the hipsnap so that your face remains in or near the water, and simultaneously swing your assist hand across the kayak's deck. Continue to drive with your knee until the kayak is fully upright.

in the water until your head swivels onto the deck of the kayak. This allows you to keep your entire support arm and hand in the water throughout the hipsnap, giving maximum purchase. When you become proficient with the forward lean, try completing the roll with a pure side lean, you'll find it almost as easy.

6. **The Recovery Following the Hipsnap Is Not a Separate Action—It Is a Result of Doing the Hipsnap and Lean Correctly**. A common mistake during the recovery is to leave your head and both arms over the edge of the boat. This terminates the roll prematurely because the boat will strike your chest and left arm, leaving much of your weight over the water, not the boat. Instead, allow your body to smoothly move onto the top of the kayak by swinging your assist hand across the deck as soon as the hipsnap nears completion that is, as your head begins to move toward the kayak's rail (figure 10.1 e). This not only gets the assist hand out of your way, it dramatically improves balance. Initially, try to overshoot the body-swivel onto the kayak by swinging your body all the way across the deck to the other side. This will eliminate mechanical and mental blocks to spinning your kayak fully upright.

A Method for Learning the Hands Roll

You'll need the following to learn this roll: an assistant with a boat, a spare flotation jacket, and two ping pong paddles (plastic plates, frisbees, or webbed gloves as in figure 10.2 will do). First, smooth out your forward lean by repeating the exercise shown in figure 5.4, but lean forward instead of backward. Then, repeat the hipsnap exercises described in chapter 6 to be certain your hipsnap is smooth, fast, and you have no head-lifting tendencies. Use your assistant's hands just below the water level or the bow of another boat for support, and complete your hipsnaps leaning forward. Keep your head down until the boat's cockpit rim forces it up, place as little pressure on your support hand as possible, and finish by swinging your assist hand across the deck for balance.

Next use a rolled up flotation jacket to support your hands while practicing your hipsnap and forward lean, as in figure 10.3. Place your support hand in the center of the jacket, with your assist hand resting on top of it. Stretch and push the jacket as far away from the side of the boat as possible. Then, simultaneously hipsnap, swivel your body and head forward onto the kayak, and swing your assist hand across the deck for balance. Leave your face in the water until your head rides up onto the

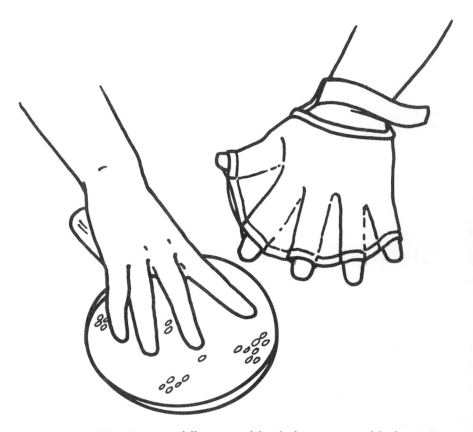

Figure 10.2: Ping Pong paddles or webbed gloves give added support when learning hands rolls.

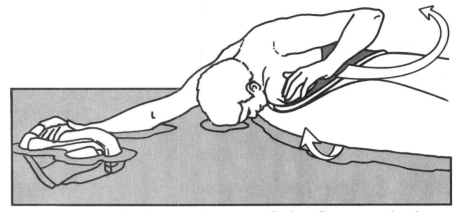

Figure 10.3: Hands roll practice using a rolled up flotation jacket for support.

front deck. The jacket will sink a little during this maneuver, but not a lot if you do the hipsnap well.

When you execute the hipsnap well using a flotation jacket under your hand for support, you're ready to try an exercise unique to learning the hands roll that supports your chest and leaves your hands free to move through a nearly normal range of motion. Have your assistant get in his boat and move his bow near your cockpit (a long boat with a narrow bow is best). With the boats about 45 degrees apart, lean to your right and rest your chest on his bow, the bow nestled under your armpit. With your weight supported in this way, rotate your boat upside down as in figure 10.4 a. Lay your support arm and hand on the surface of the water and your assist hand on the deck. This is nearly the position you would be in after reaching to the surface during a hands roll, just before the hipsnap.

You can now practice a powerful hipsnap with both hands free. During the hipsnap, use your abdominal muscles to pull your bow toward the other boat's cockpit. This abdominal tightening allows you to swing your head and chest forward smoothly onto the front deck. Your boat will back away from your assistant's boat during the hipsnap permitting your support hand to move smoothly from the surface through an arc ending under your boat, as in figure 10.4 b, and to fully support the last part of your hipsnap in the process. Remember to throw your assist hand across your own bow for balance.

The preceding exercises should help to iron out any catches or snags in your developing hands roll from the hipsnap to the recovery. Now let's concentrate on getting you from the setup position into a position from which you can start your hipsnap. This is a task dependent upon your being oriented to both your boat and the surface of the water. To do this, start from the setup position and swing your hands up and onto your assistant's hands, held about six inches under the surface of the

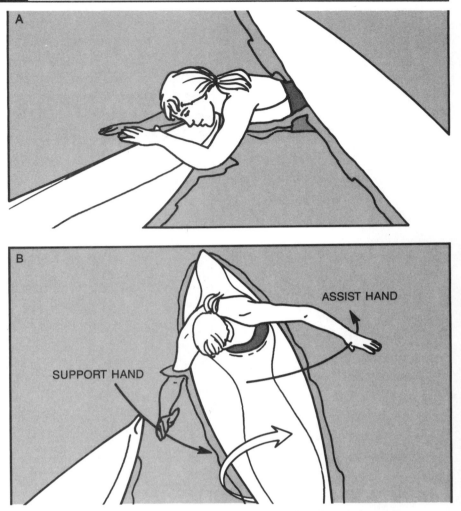

Figure 10.4 a,b: Hands roll practice using another boat's bow for support. A Initially support yourself by resting your armpit on the very end of the bow of your assistant's boat. Hold your support arm near the surface. B This allows you to practice and coordinate the motions of the second half of the hands roll. It's a risk-free way to discover how much your hand and arm will support you during a quick hipsnap.

water and 1.5 feet from the boat. Then pause to make certain that you are looking downward, and that both hands are palm downward (a position similar to that shown in figure 6.3). If they are, hipsnap the boat completely upright, keeping your head in the water while you swivel forward onto the deck. Leave your support hand on your assistant's hands, and place as little pressure on it as possible. Repeat this maneuver with the goal of completely removing the pause between the upward reach and hipsnap.

You're now ready to try the complete roll on your own holding a ping-pong paddle, or wearing webbed gloves in both hands. The additional support allows you to complete the roll with less than perfect timing or technique. It's a good idea to have an assistant ready to support your chest during the first several attempts. Start in the setup position and begin the roll by leaning briskly up to the surface toward your left side. As your hands and the top of your helmet near the surface, turn your palms down, extend your trunk away from the boat, and simultaneously execute a strong hipsnap. During the hipsnap, smoothly swivel your body forward onto the deck of the kayak, swing your left arm over the bow for balance, and allow your right arm and hand to swing in a smooth arc underneath the boat.

There is often a major mental barrier to overcome at this point. Although you may have perfect technique and minimal pressure on your hands when something or someone gives your hands solid support, there is a tendency to push down strongly with your hands when you attempt to do the roll on your own. This is probably because you try to feel some resistance against your hand before you hipsnap, a sensation that won't occur during a hands roll. Trust that your hands-arm-chest platform gives you adequate purchase to do the hipsnap. Ignore your hands after your reach to the surface, and concentrate on the hipsnap. When you can complete the roll consistently, try to roll with a glove or Pong-Pong paddle in only your support hand. Finally, try to roll using only your hands.

■ Ignore your hands after your reach to the surface, and concentrate on the hipsnap.

Once you learn one version of the hands roll you can play with and learn many others, knowing you have one reliable way to right your boat. Most variations differ only in their means of bringing hands and arms to the surface before the hipsnap. A sculling hands roll is obviously inefficient but may challenge you: use a sculling motion with both hands to move your upper body toward the surface and to obtain purchase for the hipsnap. This roll is relatively easy to do in the pool if you lean strongly toward the surface and invest your energy in the hipsnap (you can't shove your hands downward when sculling upward). You'll find a one-hand roll more difficult than the two-hands roll because it achieves purchase with just the support hand, which can't reach as close to the surface without help from your assist hand. An advantage of the one-hand roll is that you can practice it and still hold your paddle in your free hand. If you have difficulty, you can paddle roll upright.

The Two-Stroke Hands Roll

There is one more forward-leaning hands roll I like to describe, my personal favorite, which I call a two-stroke hands roll, shown in figure 10.5. This technique is more complex than the two-handed hands roll because the hipsnap is timed to coincide with extension of the second

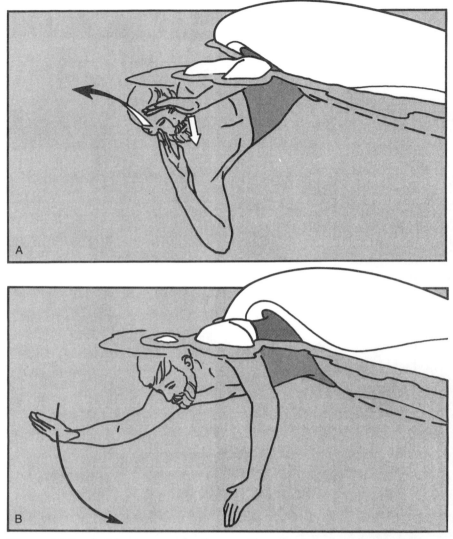

Figure 10.5 a,b: The two-stroke forward-leaning hands roll. A Reach as high toward the surface with your support hand as possible, while using your assist hand to help push you upward. B Your support hand turns palm downward during this reach. Begin a quick hipsnap at the moment your hand is nearest the surface.

hand during a two-stroke roll. This roll makes much better use of the assist hand to bring your head and outboard hand to the surface before the hipsnap. I think this makes it more reliable than any one- or two-handed hands roll on whitewater.

Begin this roll like previous hands rolls by moving your head and trunk toward the surface directly to the side and away from the kayak (toward your left hand for a right-handed roll). This time, however, the initial upward movement of your head is improved by stroking from the surface downward with the assist hand (figure 10.5 a). As your head approaches the surface, reach up and outward with your support hand, and turn it palm down (figure 10.5 b). If you've done a good job so far, the fingers of your right hand and the top of your head may break the

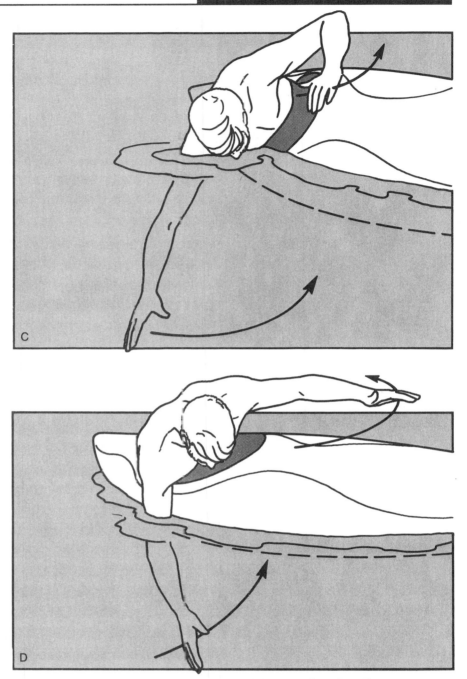

Figure 10.5 c,d: The two-stroke forward leaning hands roll. C Lean forward and swing your assist hand across the deck as the kayak rolls underneath you. D A forward-leaning hands roll allows you to sweep your hand through a large arc, completely under the kayak.

surface slightly. The way your support hand replaces your assist hand at the surface is similar to a swimming side stroke.

Your hipsnap should start about the time your support hand approaches the surface and your palm and both shoulders turn downward. This is when the surface area of the "platform" you use to support your hipsnap has reached its peak. Execute the hipsnap and recovery in the same manner as the two-handed roll.

Backward-Leaning Hands Rolls

For several years I could only do forward-leaning hands rolls. I thought that one hands roll was pretty much like any other, and I could see no advantage in learning a backward-leaning roll. Then one day I saw another kayaker twirl his paddle in his right hand while rolling upside down, pass the paddle through the air to his left hand, and roll upright with his left hand continuing the paddle twirl. That became the elusive goal that motivated me to learn backward-leaning hands rolls. It took much more work than I expected to train my body to lean backward instead of forward, but backward is the only way to go if you want to paddle twirl during a roll (for those of you concerned with such useless trivia). More seriously though, backward-leaning hands rolls are useful tools that I feel are sometimes more effective than forward-leaning rolls on whitewater, as I discuss in chapter 17.

The Two-Handed, Backward-Leaning Hands Roll

This roll is similar to the two-handed forward-leaning hands roll, except you angle the initial side lean toward the stern, and the roll is completed with a strong backward lean, swiveling your head and back onto the top of the stern deck (figure 10.6). It ends with the paddler looking skyward, head resting on the back deck and arms extended over the water on either side of the kayak. Allow your bottom to rise up out of the seat at the

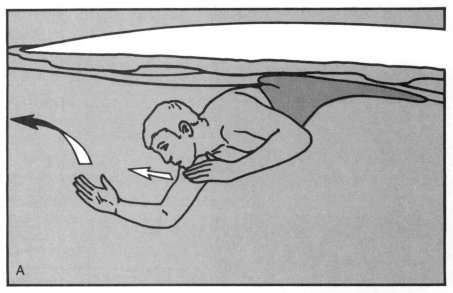

Figure 10.6 a: The two-handed back leaning hands roll. A Leave the tucked forward setup position and lean strongly upward, and somewhat toward the stern. Drive your head and both hands toward the surface.

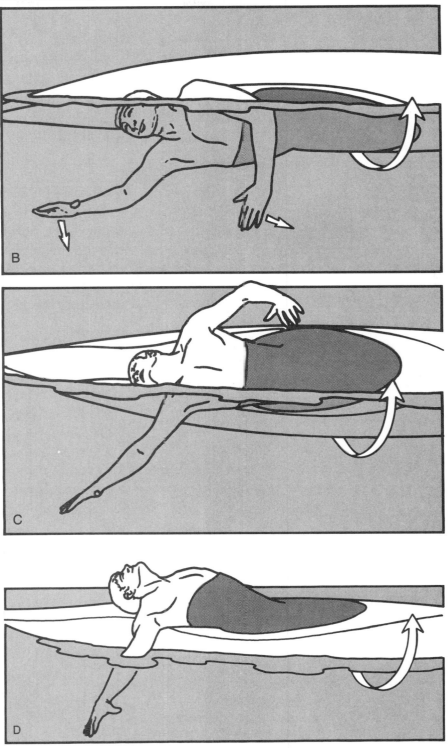

Figure 10.6 b-d: The two-handed backleaning hands roll. B Powerfully hipsnap the boat when full extension of your hands and trunk is reached. C A strong backward lean accompanies the hipsnap, and moves your head onto the stern deck. D The assist hand is swung quickly to the opposite side of the boat which helps move your shoulders squarely over the top of the stern deck and restores balance.

completion of the roll, making the extreme backward lean considerably easier.

The assist hand gives less support during this roll than during its two-handed forward-leaning counterpart, because it is quickly withdrawn from the water and swung to the other side of the boat during the back lean. You will use the assist hand to far better advantage during a two-stroke backward-leaning technique.

The Two-Stroke, Backward-Leaning Hands Roll

This roll, or one very similar to it, is the one I most often see used by hands-paddling playboaters (figure 10.7). In my opinion, it is more powerful than any other hands roll. A downward stroke with the assist hand during the initial side lean moves your head, chest, and support hand toward the surface and toward the stern rail (figure 10.7 a). The early backward lean allows the second hand stroke to begin near the surface, with your head very close to the stern deck (figure 10.7 b). The two hand strokes are done quickly; the hipsnap beginning with the second stroke (figure 10.7c).

This is an improvement on the forward-leaning two-stroke roll, because the first hand stroke passing downward in front of your face prevents an early forward lean toward the boat's rail, but does not prevent an early backward lean throughout this first stroke. Starting the second stroke with your head near the boat's rail reduces the work needed to roll upright, and makes this technique highly effective.

In calm water I like doing a slower, smoother version of this roll which feels quite different, although any illustration would look similar to figure 10.7. The timing more closely resembles a sweep paddle roll than a brace roll, in that hip rotation begins during the first downward stroke and continues throughout the second, blending into the overall backward lean until the head and trunk swivel onto the stern deck. The assist hand supports this early hip rotation in a manner similar to the early sweeping blade of the sweep roll. I try to keep my head moving smoothly in one direction only from bow to stern deck, and so avoid the sensation of moving first strongly upward, and then in toward the boat during the hipsnap. This way of doing the two-stroke backward leaning roll is slower and probably less effective in whitewater than the brisk, more overtly powerful version described above; but it feels nearly effortless, like swimming your way to the surface with two well-placed, well-timed crawl strokes.

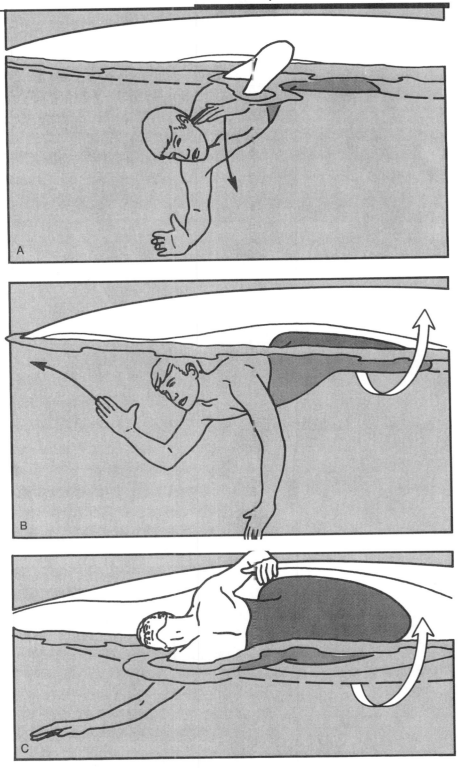

Figure 10.7 a-c: The two-stroke backward-leaning hands roll. The first half of this roll is similar to the forward-leaning version, but the initial lean away from the boat is more toward the stern. It's completed with a pronounced back lean (see figure 10 7 d on the next page).

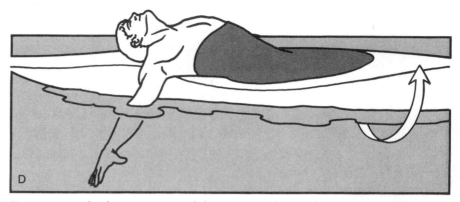

Figure 10.7 d: The recovery of the two-stroke backward-leaning hands roll.

The No-Hipsnap Roll—an Exercise

During any backward-leaning hands roll, you should swivel your head and back smoothly onto the center of the stern deck, touching the deck with your head. You can refine that backward lean and practice a strong two stroke motion with your hands by doing an exercise I call a "no-hipsnap" roll, shown in figure 10.8. It takes some courage, but you will grease your backward-leaning hands roll if you can do it. Do *not* use this roll in whitewater because it uses only arm and shoulder strength to roll the boat, it's not reliable, and offers no protection to your face.

To do the no-hipsnap roll, lie with your back and head resting on your kayak's stern. Lean far enough to the side to tip the boat upside down but immediately return to the backward lean position, head firmly held against the stern of the boat and looking straight down in the water. You should be able to touch the surface of the water with the finger tips of both hands, as in figure 10.8 a. This roll is feasible only if you keep all your weight close to the roll axis of the boat. *Keep your head in contact with the stern deck at all times!*

■ This roll is feasible only if you keep all of your weight close to the roll axis of the boat.

Initially, have a helper place his hand under one of yours for support, let's say your left hand. When you have rotated the kayak halfway using your helper's hands as support, replace your left hand with your right hand to finish the roll (figure 10.8 b). Keep your arms straight while they are sweeping, and remember to move your left hand across your chest to the opposite side of the boat as the roll nears completion (figure 10.8 c). You should be looking straight up at the sky again (figure 10.8 d). No more than light pressure on your helper's hands is needed to roll the boat, and you should be able to do this slowly and without strain.

When you can manage the assisted rolls easily, and have figured out which direction you'll need to turn and which way is up, try rolling without

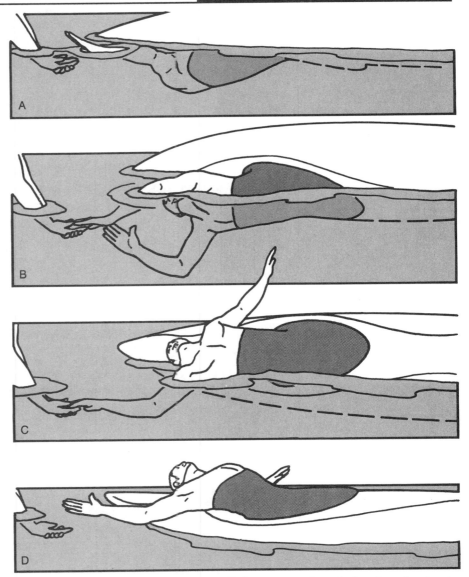

Figure 10.8 a-d: The no-hipsnap roll—keep your head glued to the back deck of your kayak! After learning the arm and body movements with the aid of an assistant, try it without assistance. This is a practice maneuver only; do not try this roll in whitewater!

assistance using ping-pong paddle blades or webbed gloves, and then only with your bare hands. You'll have to move your arms very quickly to do the roll unassisted, unlike the practice runs.

The One Hand, Backward-Leaning Hands Roll

This roll is similar to the forward-leaning version except instead of initially leaning to the side, you lean sideways, backward and upward to the rear corner of the kayak. When arm extension is greatest and your support hand is nearest the surface, do a powerful hipsnap and swing your back and head quickly onto the stern deck. Although I was slow to learn this technique, it's popular with playboaters; and it's a hands roll you can practice still holding onto your paddle for emergency backup support. The paddle, held in your free hand, may actually improve your balance if you initially keep its weight over the kayak (figure 10.9 a-c).

When you've developed a reliable hands roll on one side, learn its mirror-image counterpart on the opposite side. Hands rolls rapidly become ambidextrous, which is a good thing because in whitewater it's very easy to forget which side is your "on-side."

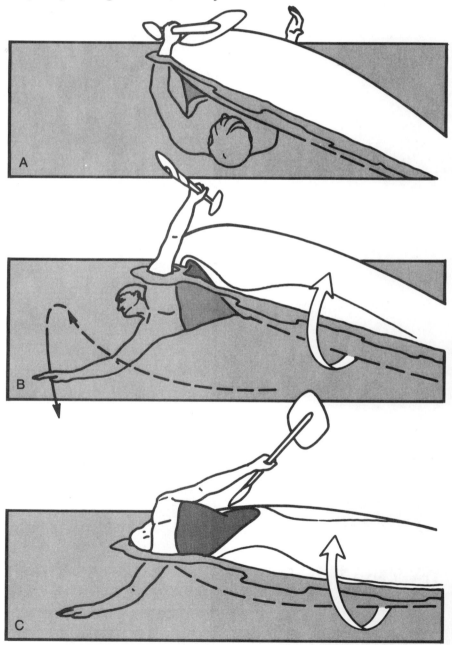

Figure 10.9 a-c: The one-hand back-leaning hands roll. Use the paddle as a balancing aid.

Hands Paddling

I will start this section off with a cautionary note. Hands paddling is fun; however, it is not something I choose to do while running difficult whitewater. I only hands paddle under safe controlled conditions in the pool or on the river. The power that can be generated with your hands as compared to that with a paddle is infinitesimally small. My paddle is one of the most important pieces of safety gear I carry, and I wouldn't attempt to kayak anything potentially dangerous without it.

Hands paddling, although not itself a basic skill, teaches basic skills—boat control skills that are not esoteric or ultra-advanced boating technique. You *must* relinquish dependence on your paddle to learn how to use boat control as your primary playboating tool. This occurs most rapidly when you dare to hands paddle. Mastery of even one hands roll will significantly improve your self-confidence. This leads to a willingness to experiment with familiar whitewater maneuvers while holding your paddle in reserve, or going entirely without it. Hands paddling quickly teaches you to stop fighting the current because you have voluntarily given up your chief means of doing that. You can then learn how to encourage the river to do most of your work for you—work that you would otherwise have done yourself, unconsciously and unnecessarily, using paddle strokes.

Balance and Bracing

Once you have a reliable hands roll, you'll be able to experiment with a diversity of hand strokes. You'll quickly learn that a forward or backward lean improves balance and is extremely useful when hands paddling. As your head moves closer to the deck, it also moves closer to the water and toward the roll axis of the boat, which lowers your center of gravity and adds to stability. Equally important, the closer to the deck you lean, the more of your arm and hand can enter the water, giving much better purchase. Learn to lean forward (nose to deck) when off-balanced, holding your hands ready to brace if needed.

See how far you can tilt the boat over and still brace upright with your hand and arm. If you keep your head on the forward deck, touching it, you should be able to tilt the boat over nearly 90 degrees and still regain your balance with a hands brace. A hipsnap isn't possible in this forward-leaning position, so this brace works very much like the no-hipsnap roll; it uses only hand and arm power. Fortunately, as you've already seen with the no-hipsnap roll, when your body weight is close to the roll axis of the boat, the kayak can be easily rolled using only hand power.

Forward, Back and Turning Strokes

Try stroking forward with both hands at the same time and also alternating your hands, as if you were swimming a crawl stroke. Do the same paddling backward. You'll find backward strokes are much more powerful than forward strokes because you can get your shoulders and trunk behind each stroke (figure 10.10 a).

Turn the forward-moving kayak by leaning forward and reaching

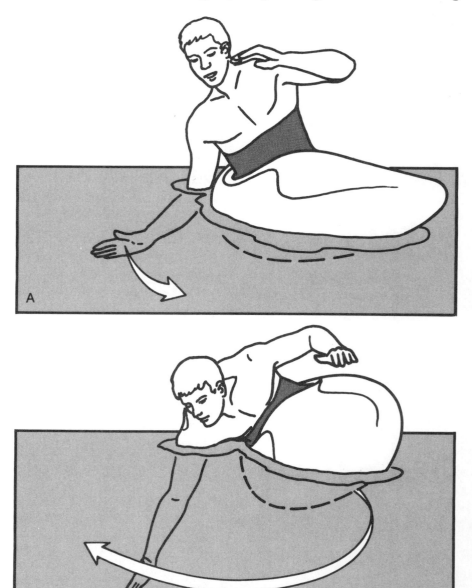

Figure 10.10 a,b: A Backward hand strokes are much stronger than forward hand strokes because they make better use of the powerful muscles of your trunk. B This picture shows how to pivot the forward moving kayak around your arm—it's a little like swinging yourself around a flagpole.

into the water with your palm toward the bow. The boat will pivot around your arm in much the same way you might swing yourself around a flagpole (figure 10.10 b).

Sustained Brace Strokes

Sculling strokes are useful when recovering from a marginal hands roll. Use a rapid back and forth motion of your hand, turning your palm in the direction your hand is moving, much as you turned the power face of your paddle when sculling. Try holding your boat on edge using a rapid hand sculling motion for support.

Hands paddling and hands rolls are instructive and incredibly fun; I encourage you to learn these skills early in your paddling experience. Beginners do remarkably well balancing without their paddles. On day one, many can hands paddle holding an edge up. On day two many can balance and maintain edge control when pushed across a well-defined eddy line. Without a paddle to lean upon for support, they are much less likely to lean away from the boat.

■ Any maneuver that can be done without a paddle will result in a smoother, more effective paddle technique.

Bryan Tooley calls hands paddling the "great debugger." Any maneuver that can be done without a paddle will result in a smoother, more effective paddle technique. It's helpful to have had enough experience to remain oriented to the surface and your boat when upside down before you learn a hands roll, but don't wait until you have perfected your paddle roll. Learn the hands roll to improve your paddle roll. The boat control demonstrated in even a poorly performed hands roll almost guarantees a highly effective whitewater paddle roll. Hands paddling skills you learn on flat water will lead to increased paddling efficiency, smoothness, stability, and balance on whitewater.

Part II
- An Introduction to Playboating

When you bicycle, you take for granted the bicycle's stability; its tires are resting on the ground. If you remain balanced, the bicycle remains upright. A surfing kayak behaves in a more complex manner, it can suddenly flip in whitewater, even though you sit upright with your weight directly over the center line of the boat. Stability cannot be assumed. Simple comparisons with any other craft or vehicle break down when you consider the kayak routinely moves backward, sideways, pitches up and down, tilts, and rolls. So let's build from scratch a kayaker's concept of balance and stability.

Stability refers to the kayak's tendency to remain upright. When resting on flat water or moving at the same speed as the current, no outside forces affect the boat—it behaves very predictably. If your weight remains over the kayak and not off to one side, the boat remains stable and upright.

When the kayak is moving across the current, or the current is moving under a nearly stationary kayak (the usual situation when bow- or side-surfing), tremendous dynamic forces are at work on the kayak's hull. As long as you position your edges so that river current flows under the hull, this water will tend to lift the kayak and keep it upright. *The kayak remains stable only as long as you hold your upstream edge out of the current with a lifted knee,* as shown in figure 11.1 a.

Acquire stability in the same way when doing eddy turns, except now the kayak is moving rapidly while the water in the eddy is relatively still or moving in a direction opposite to the main current. The kayak, as

■ When the kayak is moving across current, tremendous dynamic forces are at work on the kayak's hull.

Figure 11.1 a: Here, a side-surfing kayaker holds his upstream edge out of the current. Current flows under the kayak and supports the downstream rail.

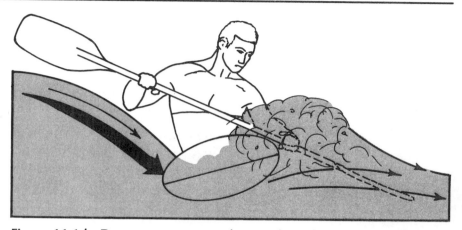

Figure 11.1 b: Drop your upstream knee side-surfing, and you ask for trouble. . . This fellow is about to be slammed upside down.

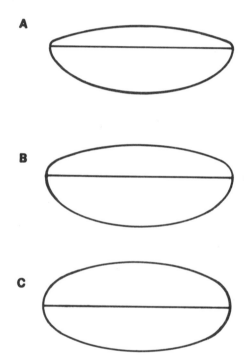

Figure 11.2 a-c: Sharp vs. round edges. The less rounded your edges, the more grabby and tippy your boat will feel in whitewater—until you learn to hold the upstream edge out of the water. These figures show different possible cross sections of a kayak. The shape of any boat can vary markedly along its length. For instance, it may be "edgy" near the ends and round in the center. The character and behavior of your boat depends on its shape.

it moves out of the current and into the eddy, experiences an onrush of water striking its downstream hull. You anticipate this effect by lifting the downstream rail with your knee when entering eddies.

You can coax a surfing kayak into spinning 360 degrees on the crest of a wave or hole as long as your edges are shifted (you lift the new upstream rail with your knee) when current first strikes each new upstream side of the boat. Allow an upstream edge to dip into the current, however, and it will be forced under water (see figure 11.1 b). More than likely, you'll suddenly and violently flip upside down.

Stability, therefore, is primarily a function of how well you control your boat's edges. Very edgy boats (those with narrow angular rails, as shown in figure 11.2 a) tend to grab and catch in the current, unless you anticipate needed edge shifts as you maneuver about the river and do them with split-second timing. Kayaks with blunt or rounded edges are far more forgiving because their rails tend to shed water and respond sluggishly to minor or momentary current flow across the deck. Most playboaters, myself included, prefer blunt edges; but those who are quick and technically proficient sometimes prefer the responsiveness and performance of an edgy boat.

Hold your upstream edge out of the current, and your kayak can be considered a stable platform upon which you balance to keep your weight over the boat. Your first priority is always to achieve stability through edge control. Your second priority is to remain in balance. A good rule of thumb when playboating is to maintain edge control and balance by pulling your upstream knee up and leaning your upper body in toward that knee to keep your head over the deck, as shown in the illustrations for chapter 2 and in figure 11.1 a.

Beginners are often told to lean downstream to keep the boat stable. Unfortunately, this statement blurs the distinction between body lean and edge control. Most of the time you can, and should, control your edges while maintaining an upright posture. Sitting upright allows you to see

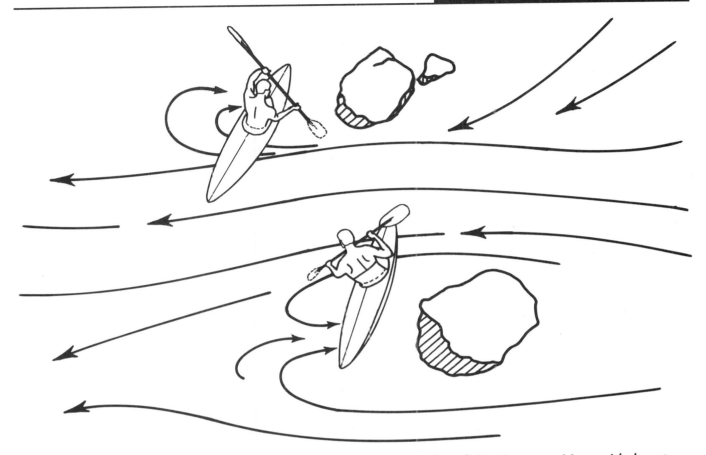

Figure 11.3: Peel-outs and eddy turns are the most common examples of situations requiring a side lean to maintain balance.

better and maintain better balance than when leaning downstream. It allows you to shift your edges quickly and lean in response to eddy lines, waves, or cross-currents. Furthermore, an upright posture often allows you to take full strokes on the "uphill" side of a kayak on edge, which can increase your stroke rate, power, and directional control. A good example of this might be your need to do an urgent and powerful upstream ferry in fast current to avoid a huge hole materializing downstream.

An upright posture is the general rule, but side leans are important in two situations. The first situation occurs whenever the kayak encounters a large change in current direction that rapidly accelerates or decelerates the boat. A momentary side lean may be needed to prevent the boat from accelerating or decelerating out from under you, allowing your body to fall unsupported into the water. Common examples of this, shown in figure 11.3, are a momentary upstream lean when entering an eddy (the boat slows or stops rapidly), and a momentary downstream lean when leaving an eddy to rejoin the river (the boat is abruptly pushed downstream as you "peel out" into the downstream current).

The second situation occurs when anything slows or stops your kayak's downstream movement in the main current, such as a hydraulic, rock, or tree. These necessitate an immediate lean downstream onto the obstacle, an action directly opposite to most beginners' instincts. Since a sudden deceleration will throw your body to the downstream side, just as it does during an eddy turn, many paddlers want to lean upstream away from the obstacle. The problem with this is that unlike the current flow in an eddy, the river's main current will continue to flow strongly past your slowed or stopped boat. An upstream lean guarantees that water will smash into your upstream rail and flip you upside down. In the case of a rock or tree, this might be a lethal one-way trip ending in a pin

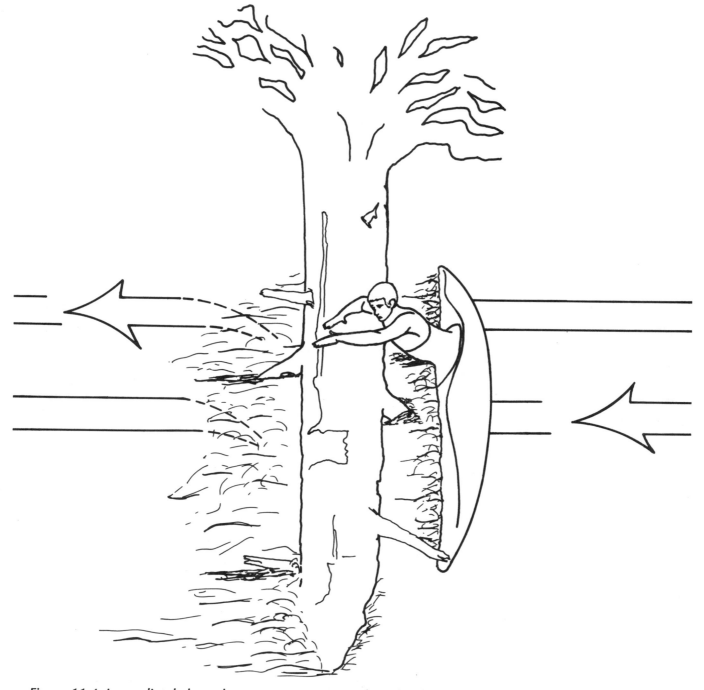

Figure 11.4: Immediately lean downstream onto any obstacle obstructing your path. This will hold your upstream edge well out of the water and keep you from being flipped upstream.

underneath the obstacle. By allowing your body to fall downstream you can brace or support your body against the obstacle, and simultaneously lift your upstream rail to ensure that the kayak does not flip (figure 11.4).

A similar situation may occur when drifting downstream sideways into a large wave (one with a nearly vertical wave face). It's a good idea to lean into this wave as if you were attacking it (figure 11.5 a), because a less pronounced lean, as seen in figure 11.5 b, may not keep your weight over the boat, and will allow your upstream edge to be caught by river current. If you hit a wave sideways and punch through it, a downstream brace easily helps you to regain your balance.

A forward lean (and, less commonly, a backward lean) will lower your center of gravity, making the boat much less tippy. Forward and backward leans may improve boat control by weighting or unweighting the kayak's bow or stern. When leaving an eddy, a backward lean helps the bow easily ride up and over a high eddy wall. Maintaining the backward lean causes the stern to be pushed downstream faster than the bow, helping to maintain an upstream ferry angle. A forward lean causes the bow to bury itself somewhat when turning into small eddies, thus tightening the turn.

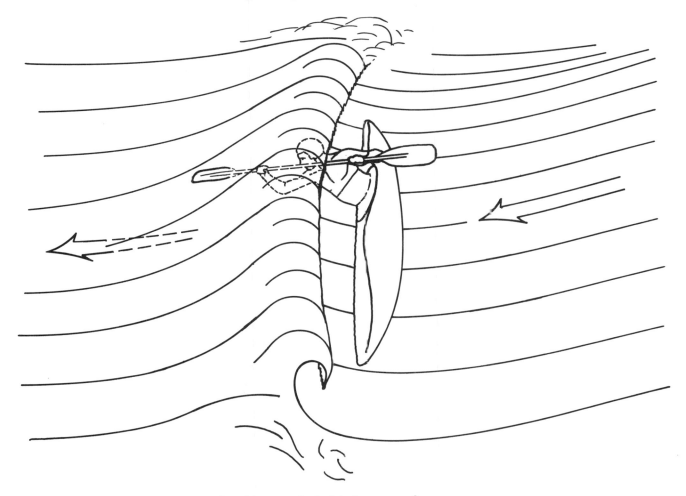

Figure 11.5 a: The right way. Lean hard into an intimidating wave face.

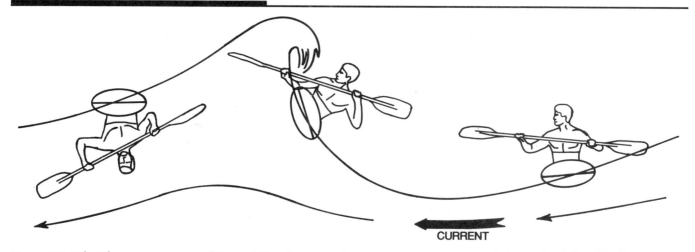

CURRENT

Figure 11.5 b: The wrong way. This paddler does not have an aggresive enough lean; he falls off balance and is flipped upside down by the current.

You will rapidly gain confidence on the river when you begin to use edge control and lean consciously and aggressively to increase your boat's stability. In a short while, you'll find yourself using appropriate edge shifts and a relaxed (usually upright) paddling posture unconsciously, and brace strokes to keep the boat right-side-up will be needed only occasionally.

OK, how do you learn edge control and balance on whitewater? The best way is to take advantage of every situation in which you can safely kayak holding your paddle out of the water (in reserve). Start with simple ferries. Practice these where there are two eddies on either side of the river, separated by swiftly moving current. Paddle strongly upstream in one eddy in order to cross the eddy line quickly and enter the current with a ferry angle that will take you across the river into the opposite eddy. The objective is to do this without taking a stroke after you leave the eddy, or to use as few paddle strokes as possible.

Leave the eddy with a strong forward stroke on the downstream side of the boat. If you punch through the eddy line with the correct angle, the boat will not be turned downstream and you will remain about even with the eddy as the kayak moves out into the current. The faster the current, the less your ferry angle should be (the more upstream the bow of your kayak should be aimed). Sit upright to maintain balance; little if any downstream lean will be needed if you hold the upstream edge out of the current.

Look carefully at the stretch of river you plan to ferry across. Small waves, when present, can be used to extend your glide. Any upstream obstructions or change in water depth may transiently slow the current and turn the kayak upstream slightly. Anticipate this by decreasing your edge tilt, or you are liable to tip over onto your downstream side when you enter the slower water. The current will support the downstream edge of the boat better in fast current than in slow, so you should increase the tilt of your boat when re-entering faster water.

See how far you can stretch your no-paddle ferries. Choose eddies that are further apart than those you've chosen before—20, 30 feet or more. Think of it as you would a long-distance golf putt. You have to peel out at the right angle and with enough speed to accommodate irregularities in the current and small turns of your kayak, and still be able to drop into your eddy on the far side of the river.

The next thing to try is drifting downstream on Class II or Class III water without using your paddle except to avoid rocks and large holes, and for an occasional brace. Sit upright on the crests of waves to get a good view, but in the troughs where current can play across your boat's edges, lean forward toward the deck to lower your center of gravity and improve stability. When drifting with the current remain relaxed and allow the kayak's edges to tilt with the contours of the waves while you remain balanced and sitting upright over the boat. You may feel more comfortable initially keeping the kayak pointed downstream, but soon you'll graduate to a full drift, allowing the kayak to turn whichever way it wants. Frequently look downstream when drifting backward so that you can anticipate lean and edge shifts that will be needed, and to avoid rocks.

When the kayak begins to drop into a small hole or hydraulic, the downstream edge will drop while the upstream edge rises. This works fine to maintain the stability of your boat; hold it on edge and remain sitting upright to maintain balance, as shown in figure 11.6. Because the boat assumes the stable position you want it to have when it enters hydraulics, you'll soon react instinctively when drifting backward, even though you don't know for sure which way the boat will turn. As one edge or the other "bites" into a hydraulic, you'll find your shoulders are thrown slightly to

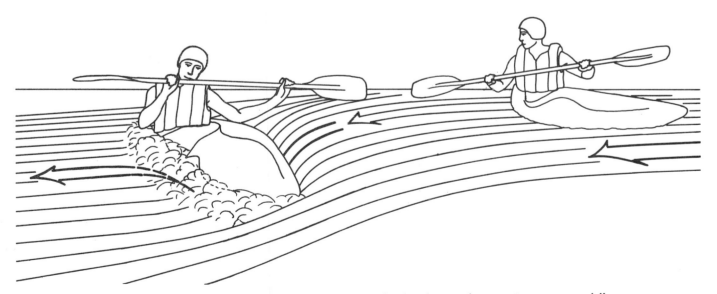

Figure 11.6: Drift practice. Try to ride out waves and small hydraulics without using your paddle.

the downstream side, and that your paddle (held in reserve) is automatically ready to brace on that side. As the kayak washes through the hydraulic, the upstream edge can again be lowered, and a relaxed posture resumed.

Even though you will occasionally need to brace, do so as little as possible. Try to ride out even large edge tilts by leaning tightly into the boat and using your paddle only for balance. Free yourself from a blind reliance on your paddle to stay upright.

When you use body lean and edge control to maintain balance and achieve stability, the tremendous power available in your paddle is free to be employed to make the kayak go where you want it to go, and to do what you want it to do.

The usual entrance requirement for paddling class IV rivers is a "bombproof" roll. This is not something that can be demonstrated on flat water, even though there is no technical difference between most whitewater and flat water rolls. It has to do with your ability to roll upright consistently when large waves, cross-currents, holes, and rocks play upon you and your kayak. It has to do with keeping a cool head, good timing, and understanding the forces acting upon your boat. The following suggestions should help you successfully roll under combat conditions.

Rolling in Large Waves

If you flip above a train of large waves, you can feel the cadence of your boat being physically lifted upward by each successive wave, peaking on the crest of the wave, falling down the backface, settling in the trough, and lifting upward again. The one place you should not try to roll is in the trough between waves. The bow and stern of the kayak as well as your paddle will probably be under water, making the boat unresponsive and your roll difficult. Whether to roll on the upstream face of the wave before you reach the crest, or to roll on its backside is a matter of controversy, and has a lot to do with the size and nature of the whitewater being paddled.

My solution in most whitewater is to set up and wait until the boat can be felt to stop its upward rise. Here, the bow and stern will likely be

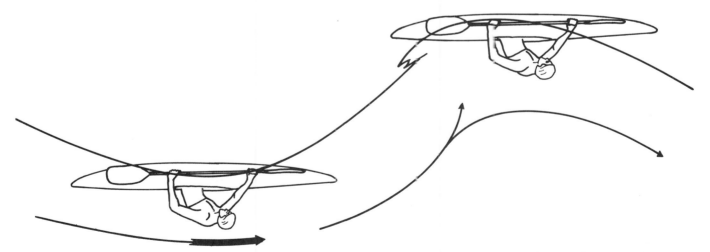

Figure 12.1: In large waves, time your roll to coincide with the top of a wave crest; this is when your boat is easiest to roll.

in the air and free of the river's influence (figure 12.1). The effect on the paddler at that moment is just like that on the driver of a car rapidly topping a rise on a country road: he feels lighter. A roll started as the boat crests a large wave is the easiest roll there is.

Rolling in Powerful Current

River current will often help you roll upright if your setup places you on the downstream side of the flipped kayak. It also may prevent the kayak from rolling fully upside down if you have to lean into the current to set up on the upstream side of the boat, as in figure 12.2. The current must be moving downstream faster than the kayak to have this effect, so it usually occurs when the boat enters current from an eddy, or washes out of a hole where it has been temporarily stopped.

Since most flips occur when the kayak catches its upstream edge in the current, a good habit to get into is to tuck and dive in the direction the kayak begins to roll. Your best bet is to maintain the rolling momentum of the kayak and immediately roll upright, planing your paddle to the surface during the sweep as soon as your body passes under the boat. This works well, even when your sweep is on the upstream side of the kayak.

If your body does not roll fully under the boat or you become disoriented, you can try patiently waiting five seconds in the setup position for the current to accelerate your kayak up to its own speed. Your paddle will then float to the surface, permitting the usual sweep and roll. If this doesn't work, or you only have seconds in which to roll upright before being filleted by rocks downstream, don't wait! Use the sweep roll or advanced brace roll to plane your blade toward the surface. If this roll attempt fails, immediately setup and roll on the opposite side, which should now be your downstream side.

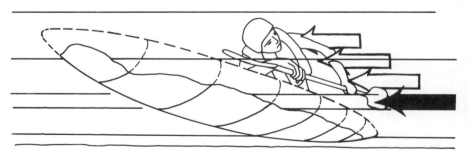

Figure 12.2: If your setup forces you to lean upstream against the current, you may not be able to bring your paddle to the surface before beginning your roll.

What Do You Do When Successive Attempts Fail?

Missed rolls often occur in situations of impending danger where a feeling of urgency, or even panic, may cause you to take shortcuts with your setup and roll. A lack of air, or being surprised by an underwater rock may lead to an urgent, abbreviated roll. Less than excellent technique will cause a missed roll in turbulent, squirrelly water such as that found along powerful eddy lines, or downstream of a waterfall or large hole where the water is aerated and offers poor paddle purchase. Fatigue or cold may be superimposed on any of these scenarios, and cause sluggish thinking and automatic, poorly thought-out actions. In this setting, I think there is a tendency to neglect the hipsnap and instead pull strongly down on the paddle. This usually results in one breath of air, and a failed roll.

I've already told you what I do . . . if my paddle blade can reach air, I carefully execute a basic brace roll and put all my energy in the hipsnap. But the real answer is to interrupt the cycle of automatic, poorly-executed rolls, and to carefully, deliberately, lean forward into the setup position. Then concentrate, and do your best roll well.

Disorientation

The last situation we'll talk about is flipping in or near a hole, and being held on the hole's perimeter by recirculating water, sort of like an upside down bow- or stern-surf. It may feel to you as if the boat is constantly moving in a violent current when, in actuality, the boat may be nearly stationary while the current swirls typhoon-like about you. Terms like "up," "down," and "surface" have no real meaning here. You can only move the paddle in relation to your kayak and the current moving across it.

Realize that doing *anything* in this situation will change the dynamics of your position, so the first thing to do is lean forward into the setup position. If you are in an inverted bow-surf, the resistance of your chest and paddle to the current as you sit forward may by itself turn the boat or wash you free of the hole.

Next, begin your normal roll, but don't expect the hyperaerated recirculating water downstream of the hole to offer your paddle a normal amount of support. Instead of depending on surface water, it's often more effective to use the current flowing past the kayak, wherever it is, to support your paddle. So as you sweep your blade, search for resistance—"listen" to what your paddle tells you. If you feel strong resistance (water pressure) against the power face of your paddle during

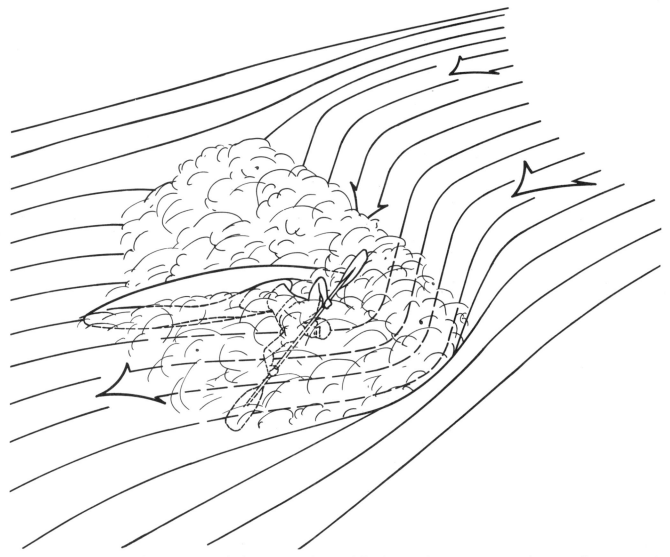

Figure 12.3: Disoriented in or near a hole? Rotate the paddle during the sweep part of your roll to create the greatest possible water pressure against the blade. Powerful current moving through the hole can give your blade purchase, and help you roll upright.

any roll, *hold the paddle in that position.* This pressure is usually generated by strong downstream currents that may dislodge the boat from the hydraulic or enable you to hipsnap upright (figure 12.3).

Therein lies the experienced paddler's secret to rolling in combat conditions in or near holes: you don't have to be oriented to the surface to roll successfully if you can feel your blade's resistance to the current as you sweep your paddle, and you turn the blade to obtain good purchase. From that point, with the river's current solidly supporting the paddle, you can usually effect a good hipsnap and a successful roll.

So when you feel disoriented or stuck, execute a good roll; feel the play of current on your paddle during the sweep and use it to your advantage. I'll talk more about this in chapter 16. I know of no shortcut to acquiring this skill, except possibly the sculling practice drills in chapter 9, which improve blade control and feel. You'll naturally acquire the knack sometime after your umpteenth whitewater roll.

13 · Bow-Surfing

Every surfing wave has its own character. Some are broad and glass smooth, requiring only a few gentle strokes to control the boat, while others demand vigorous paddling to hold the bow into the current. You can bow-surf as long as the force of gravity pulling the kayak down a wave face roughly equals the boat's resistance to water flowing up the wave face. Maintaining this delicate equilibrium requires artful piloting: directional control with just enough hull and paddle resistance in the current to keep the kayak from sliding too far forward (causing the bow to dive or "pearl"), but not so much as to drag the boat too far backward (causing you to be "blown off" the wave).

The quick reflexes and motor skills you'll need to bow-surf can be learned by practicing on small gentle waves at first, gradually working your way onto larger waves with irregular shapes and powerful current. In this chapter, I discuss how to enter a wave, control your side to side and fore and aft position, manage your edges during turns, and salvage a surf when your bow pearls.

Catching the Wave

Getting on a wave is sometimes the hardest part of surfing one. One way is to drift backward onto the wave, paddling upstream for all you're worth. It requires considerable effort in mid-current to slow the kayak's downstream movement, especially as your stern falls backward into the wave's trough; but if you paddle hard enough, the kayak will slow to a stop and begin to bow-surf as your stern rises and gravity helps you oppose the current. Remember to look over your shoulder several times to make sure you're heading for the wave and not for some point off to the side. If you can't paddle upstream forcefully enough to match the speed of the current (and skillfully enough to maintain your upstream angle), your downstream momentum will almost certainly blast you right through your wave.

A backward drift is the only way to reach some waves, such as those in the middle of the river. (The best, smoothest surfing wave in many rapids, especially in big volume whitewater, is often the first wave in midstream). Fortunately, there is often a better, easier alternative. If you can spot an eddy just upstream or adjacent to the wave you want to bow-surf, it is almost always easier to pull into this eddy letting it stop your downstream momentum, and then paddle onto your wave at leisure.

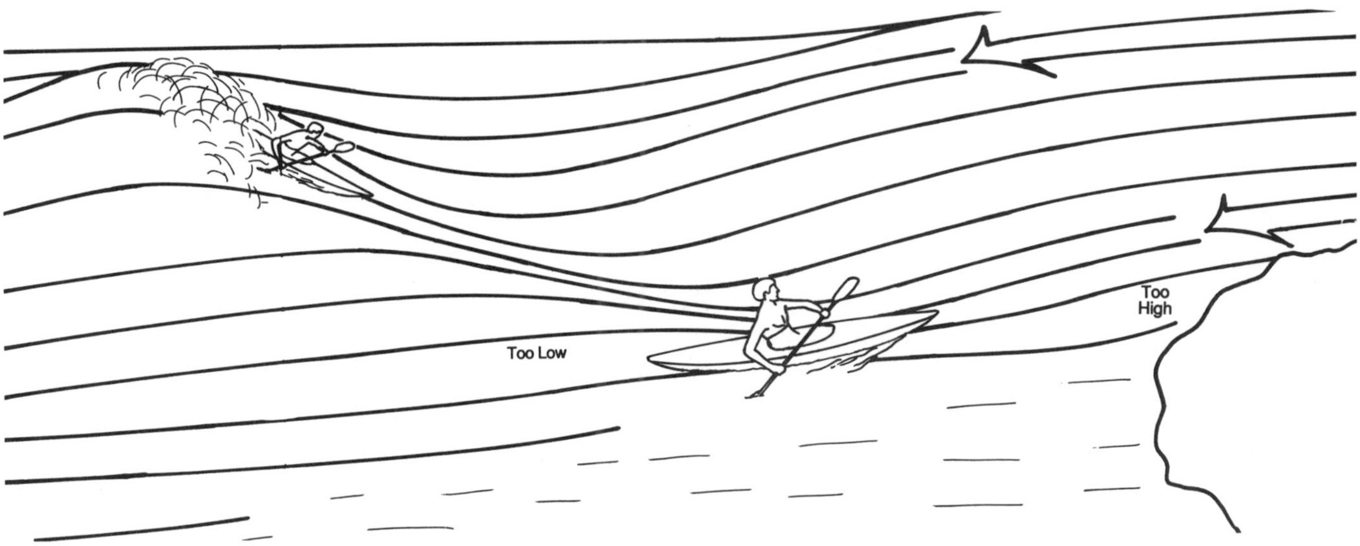

Figure 13.1: Gain access to the main wave face by surfing along its shoulder. Entering current above or below the shoulder in an attempt to ferry toward the wave is usually wasted effort.

Occasionally, when the eddy is adjacent to the main wave, you can punch through the eddy line and glide directly onto it. The vast majority of the time, however, you will need to identify and use a lateral extension of the main wave. The lateral extension, or "shoulder" is usually a small wavelet angled upstream into flatter, more slowly moving water. Reaching it may require energetic paddling, but invariably less effort than paddling onto the main wave from above or below in much faster current. Once this wavelet is reached, you can ferry/surf along it to the main wave face with little effort.

The biggest problem getting on the main wave face, especially when it is only 5 or 10 feet from the eddy, occurs because paddlers are not careful enough to see and use the wave's shoulder. An attempt to ferry onto the main wave from downstream of the shoulder in fast current usually results in a vain struggle to paddle up the wave's backface. An attempt to enter the current upstream of the shoulder, planning to slide backward onto the main wave, places the boat in fast water flowing "downhill" into the wave's trough. The kayak's downstream momentum will usually blow it through the wave. Although figure 13.1 depicts a large surfing wave, the easiest route onto any wave, large or small, is almost always along the wave's shoulder; look for it, and use it to your advantage.

Your surf onto the main wave may require forward strokes to maintain your ferry angle and position on the wave, especially on high-volume rivers where the current is fast and wave troughs are relatively wide and flat. Usually, though, you can bow-surf along the wave shoulder by gently lifting the kayak's upstream edge while applying a rudder stroke on the upstream side, as in figure 13.2. The rudder opposes the tendency of the current to push the bow downstream and controls your ferry/surf angle. Paddle hard enough through the eddy line and up to the wave's

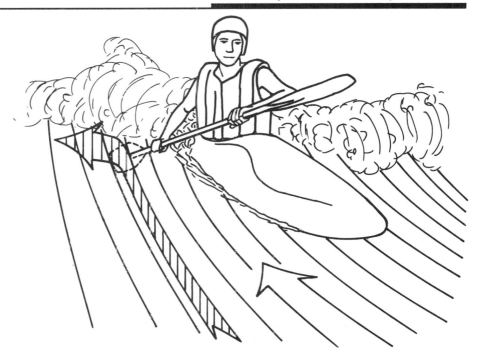

Figure 13.2: A rudder stroke directs water away from the stern of your boat. When applied on the upstream side of the kayak, as it is during a surf across a wave face, the rudder stroke keeps your boat from turning sideways in the current by keeping the bow pointed upstream.

shoulder so that you can coast onto it with your rudder stroke already in place. Lean slightly backward and enter the wave with a shallow ferry angle. You can stop your boat's travel across the wave by applying increased back pressure on your rudder, which will swing the bow upstream into a straight-on surf.

Controlling Your Bow-Surf

Staying on the wave is a matter of gentle edge control and making early small corrections with your paddle before the kayak drifts more than a few degrees off course. The key to early (and therefore easy) corrections is to identify an upstream reference point when you're surfing directly into the current; any tree or rock directly upstream of current flowing through your wave will do. Keep both your kayak's bow and the upstream landmark within your peripheral vision, as in figure 13.3 a. If you keep your bow in line with this upstream reference point, you'll tend to remain in about the same place on the wave. Whenever the bow crosses your line of sight to this upstream reference point, a rudder or sweep stroke can quickly bring it back into line, as shown in figure 13.3 b.

A common mistake is to focus attention solely on the bow of the boat and the water immediately around the bow. This makes it hard to gauge

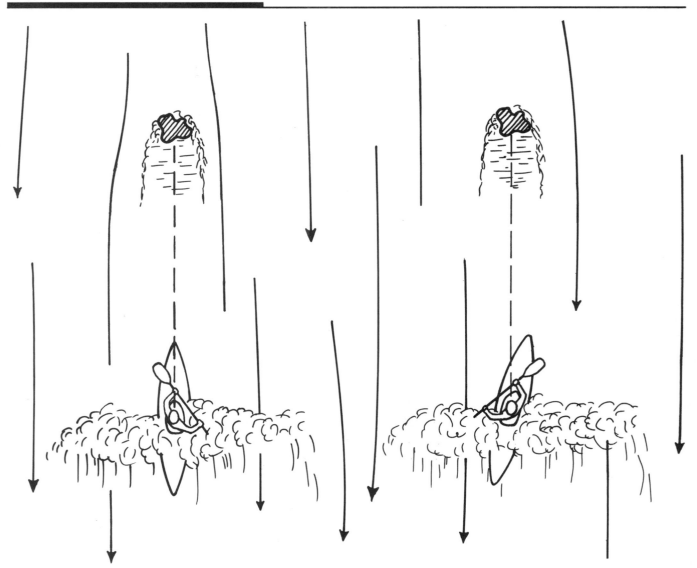

Figure 13.3 a,b: A (at left) An upstream landmark can help you to remain oriented to your position on the wave face, and it allows you to make early corrections to your bow-surfing angle. B A rudder switch is usually needed when your bow moves past your line of sight to this landmark.

the true direction of current through the wave, and delays your knowing the boat has turned off course until the error is too great to correct. We all had to learn this same sort of lesson to paddle in a straight line; extend your visual awareness to the surrounding landscape in order to know where you're going.

The usual way to hold the kayak's bow into the current as it surfs to the right and left of your reference point is to alternate rudder strokes, switching the paddle blade to each new upstream side of the boat. Beginners often find the bow swinging downstream and out of control while their blade is out of the water during the rudder switch. This occurs either because they are late in starting the rudder switch or because the paddle is moved with raised arms through a wide arc, giving the current ample time to shove the bow off to one side. It helps to keep looking straight ahead, and to move the paddle quickly back into the water by keeping your elbows low, and the paddle shaft in close to your body.

After you learn to bow-surf using rudder switches, fine-tune your technique by using the same blade to rudder in either direction. Hold the paddle shaft approximately parallel to the kayak's rail, and your blade close to the stern where it can most effectively turn the boat. Keep the upstream edge of the blade always climbing in the current by gently rotating the paddle blade a few degrees power face down when ruddering into the boat, as in figure 13.4, and a few degrees power face up when ruddering away.

One-side ruddering permits almost speed-of-thought course corrections because the controlling blade always remains in the water. Ruddering into the boat is a weaker stroke than ruddering away, so you'll need to keep the kayak within 10 to 20 degrees of course to avoid switching rudders. The technique works best on long smooth waves where the bow remains out of the water and sudden big paddle inputs can be avoided.

Figure 13.4: A 'one-side' rudder stroke directs current under the stern, and turns the kayak in a direction opposite that of a normal rudder stroke. This stroke is weaker, but complements the normal rudder nicely. Used together, they permit near instantaneous corrections in your bow-surfing angle without your lifting your paddle from the water.

Edge Control During Turns

Edge control when bow-surfing can be extremely important. The big question is: when turning upstream, should you tilt your edges and lean in the direction you want to turn, lowering your upstream knee in the process, or tilt your edges away from the turn, keeping your upstream edge up to maintain stability? The answer has to do with how much contact your bow has with the wave you are riding.

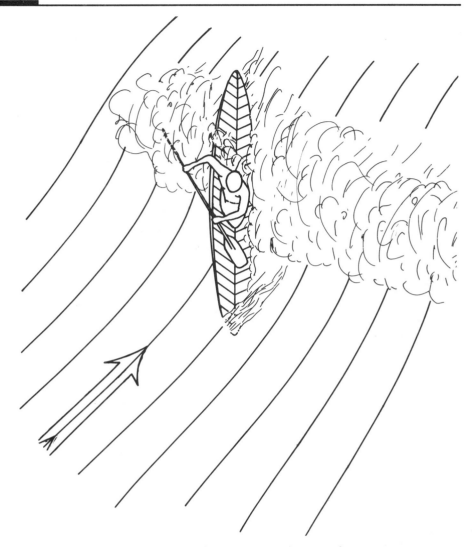

Figure 13.5 a: The paddler in figures a-c is about to begin a turn upstream to the right. The bow of this bow-surfing boat is partially under water, as is often the case when playing in low-volume creeks and streams. The upstream edge is firmly lifted throughout the initiation of the turn, which keeps current flowing under the hull and the kayak stable and upright.

On smaller volume rivers, the distance between waves is often not much greater than the length of your kayak. Since the entire kayak cannot fit easily on the wave face, it is common for the bow to partially bury in the wave trough during a bow-surf. The same thing will happen on a steep wave. Gravity will pull the kayak forward into the trough where the bow may momentarily bury in the opposing current. When your entire bow is in contact with the wave, or you bury any part of the bow during a bow-surf, it is extremely easy to catch an edge and corkscrew the boat. This is the kind of water and the type of wave most beginners learn on.

In this setting, you cannot tilt the edges of your boat upstream in the

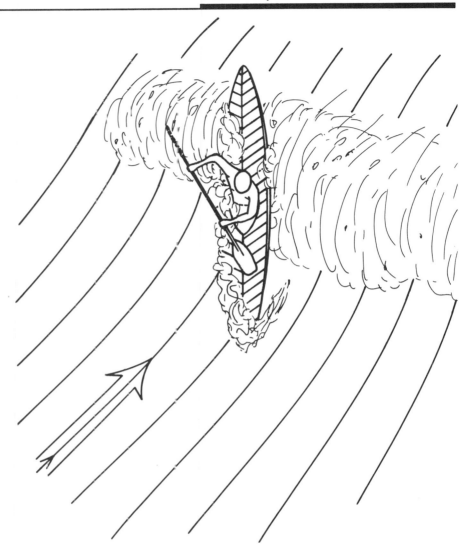

Figure 13.5 b: If the paddler in figure 13.5 A attempts instead to lean into the turn and "steer" the kayak by lifting the downstream edge, water immediately builds up on the deck, tending to sink the bow and flip the kayak. The bow is forced downstream and away from the desired turn, overwhelming the rudder stroke's ability to hold the bow up into the current.

■ You'll flip many times before you learn to suppress your instinct to lean into the turn.

direction you hope to turn and expect to do anything except turn upside down; you'll flip many times before you learn to suppress your instinct to lean into the turn. You must use only your rudder to initiate the turn, and firmly lift your upstream rail with knee pressure until the kayak is almost aligned with the current. Notice that for the first half of a left to right turn you tilt your edges to the *left* for stability—an edge shift is *not* used to steer into the turn.

Figure 13.5 a is an aerial view of a paddler surfing with a partially submerged bow. He is in the process of initiating a turn upstream with his rudder, and is lifting his upstream rail to maintain stability. If instead he attempted to "steer" into the turn by shifting his edges, you'd have the

Figure 13.5 c: The entire bow is unloaded during this surf, where the kayak is somewhat higher on the wave than in the previous two drawings. A lean into the turn helps the bow turn upstream in this situation—water pressure will build on the stern rail only. This pressure will push the stern downstream, and so pivot the bow upstream toward the desired turn.

situation in figure 13.5 b. The moment the bow's upstream edge digs into the current, tremendous pressure will build until the kayak flips or is blown off the wave.

Big volume rivers with fast water usually have wide, flat wave troughs, and the distance between waves is much longer than your kayak. During a surf on big-water waves, half or more of the bow may ride free of the water. In this setting, the kayak is insensitive to edge shifts. The upstream *stern* rail may engage the current when leaning into a turn, but this pressure *helps* turn the bow upstream by pushing the stern downstream (figure 13.5 c). There is often room to lean gently on your rudder, bank the kayak, and carve back and forth across the wave face. Big wave surfing like this gives a sensation of incredible speed and stability, as if you were piloting a jet fighter.

Controlling Your Fore and Aft Position on the Wave

Your kayak will usually find a place on the wave somewhere between the crest and the trough where *it* wants to be (depending on the speed of the current, the steepness of the wave, etc.). Now that you can get on the wave and surf it straight-on, let's look at the reasons for moving your kayak forward or backward on the wave face and how to accomplish this.

Moving backward, out of the wave trough, will decrease the likelihood of your bow pearling and veering out of control. Further back, the kayak's stern will sink into the frothy pillow at the wave's crest, making the boat more horizontal and allowing the bow to rise out of the water. The boat's edges become less sensitive to current as the bow is "unloaded," freeing the kayak to pivot in any direction. It takes good control to surf near the wave crest, but it gives you the option of paddling with velocity down the wave face toward the left, the right, or straight ahead into a pop-up. Sitting atop the crest with both the bow and stern unloaded may allow you to spin the boat 180 degrees into a stern surf.

■ **The more blade area opposing the current, the more drag is created.**

Your two means of moving backward on a wave are to increase the "drag" (resistance to current) of your paddle and that of the kayak's hull. The kayak's hull always creates drag, but this can be increased somewhat with a backward body lean. You can increase drag by converting your rudder into a sustained backstroke. Moving the blade from a position near the stern to a position even with the cockpit will decrease its rudder-like tendency to turn the boat. The more blade area opposing the current, the more drag is created.

You'll need to move forward on a wave if you're drifting backward and feel you'll lose your surf. First, get rid of all unnecessary drag. If you're still using a rudder stroke for directional control, move the blade back behind the cockpit with the paddle shaft almost parallel to the kayak (the same position as used for one-side ruddering). This will reduce drag to a minimum. Beginners often wash off small play waves because they make the mistake of pushing down and leaning on their rudder strokes without regard to how much drag they're creating with the paddle. Drag from the hull can be reduced by surfing the kayak straight ahead and using only the minimum edge tilt necessary for stability.

When removing drag fails to stabilize your surf, lean quickly forward and add in brisk, forward power strokes. If these lack sufficient "oomph", you'll find yourself teetering on the back crest of the wave in very fast current. In this situation, several rapid-fire slap strokes into the top of the wave may succeed where the usual forward stroke fails. Swing the paddle through the air at a much higher speed than before, and strike powerfully into the wave face rather than stroking through it.

Surfing With a Submerged Bow

Stable surfing with a submerged bow is possible but more difficult than when the bow is on or above the surface. Keep it as close to the surface as possible by regularly raising your upstream edge while applying an upstream rudder for support. Your bow will usually float upward when lifted on edge, because while its buoyancy remains unchanged, you reduce exposure to the downward force of the current. The bow will tend to shed water instead of impeding its flow. The upstream rudder helps back you out of the wave's trough by adding drag, turns the bow upstream, and helps you balance with the boat on edge by keeping your weight over the kayak.

The same maneuver will also work if your bow is forced suddenly deeper under the water, but it must be executed instantly and in a more pronounced fashion; otherwise you'll lose control and be forced backward off your surfing wave. Strongly lift the upstream edge, lean back, and convert your upstream rudder into a powerful back/sweep stroke. This will not only decrease pressure on the bow by backing it out of the trough, it will turn the kayak upstream, planing the "on edge" bow toward the surface in the same way a sweeping paddle with a climbing blade angle will plane or slice to the surface.

Bow-surfing a short or steep wave with a narrow trough (something half wave and half hole) will often force your bow under the water repeatedly. It takes a lot of effort to sustain your surf on these waves, but you often can by rhythmically lifting first one edge of the kayak and then the other, while alternating strong rudder strokes on each new upstream side of the kayak to control your surfing angle.

Carving Turns

Some waves simply aren't broad or flat enough to keep the bow from diving or pearling when surfed straight upstream. Increasing drag often gives only a momentary respite. The boat is likely to slide forward again if you can't find a more lasting solution like surfing over to a flatter section of the wave. You can surf some of these waves, the wider ones, by fitting your boat on them diagonally, turning, or "carving," back and forth across the wave face.

To stop your progress across the wave and reverse direction, increase your upstream rudder almost to the point of applying a backstroke. This will move the entire kayak back on the wave face, and allow the bow to clear the trough as it swings directly upstream. Change the rudder to the new upstream side as you glide forward into a controlled surf in the other direction. This transition is smooth and fast, about as fast as the time it takes to shift your weight from your right foot to your left foot and back.

You may notice from this description that a carved turn sounds very similar to the corrective stroke for a deeply submerged bow, and it is. The need to back the kayak on the wave, turn it upstream, and keep the bow from pearling is common when bow-surfing. An upstream rudder applied over a lifted upstream rail serves this purpose well. The only time you'll be able to lean into your turn and lower your upstream knee (and get away with it) is in big water where much of your bow is out of the water. The ability to carve turns rounds out your bow-surfing skills, and allows you to choose your position on the wave.

Keeping Track of Where You Are

A necessary skill, and one you'll probably pick up later than most of the others, is keeping track of where you are. Many waves flatten at the ends and are steeper in the center, but they can also vary from place to place across the wave face. Drift three feet to the left, and you'll fade off the wave imperceptibly and enter downstream current. Drift two feet to the right and you'll enter a too-steep section and possibly lose control. Try to stay where your boat is most stable until *you* decide to move it.

Initially, most paddlers focus attention on the bow of the boat and the water immediately surrounding it, but this is not enough to accurately know your position. Upstream water often looks remarkably similar, while the wave downstream (which supports your boat in a surf) changes from place to place. Learn to glance frequently to each side along the wave crest you're surfing so you can keep track of your position relative to surrounding landmarks (or watermarks, as the case may be). Only in this way will you be able to hold your boat where you want it on the wave.

If you know where you are, and accurately remember what you do, you'll probably understand why your bow-surf succeeds or fails. You'll develop an intimate knowledge of that particular wave and be better able to surf others like it. Soon, you'll *anticipate* the effect the wave and current will have on your kayak and what your responses should be; you'll avoid unnecessary movements, and your bow-surfing will become smooth and controlled.

Your goal when attempting a pop-up is not to sustain a bow-surf, but to end it as spectacularly as possible. This is accomplished by maneuvering the kayak into a position on a wave, hole, or pourover where briskly moving forward into the current will "load the deck" and force the bow deeply underwater. As deck loading occurs, the bow is pushed down and backward, forcing the kayak into a vertical position, as shown in figure 14.1. This is known as a "pop-up" or "ender." The term ender refers to one end of the boat or the other being forced under the water. If the bow is pushed downstream faster than the rest of the boat, the kayak will do a nose stand, and then cartwheel upside down. Now and then, if your balance is just right and the pop-up propels both kayak and kayaker backward at the same speed, you'll catch air *and* porpoise backward 15 or 20 feet before falling back into the water.

Mechanically speaking, the more deeply you drive the bow the more water it displaces; the more water it displaces, the stronger the forces propelling the boat back out of the water. If you've not experienced it, these forces are *powerful!* The entire boat may clear the surface during its upward trajectory! And, of course, it's not uncommon for the boat to land upside down so a good roll is essential, as with any kind of playboating.

River phenomena likely to push the bow down strongly all result from water flowing downward over ledges or large rock obstructions in the river. These include pourovers with a strong vertical chute of water, holes, and steep waves. The site you choose should be deep enough so that rocks don't block the kayak's downward movement. Not only will this interfere with pop-ups, it is likely to fold or punch holes in the bow of your boat. The quality of a given pop-up spot, in the final analysis, is determined by trial and error. On crowded rivers, finding a good spot can be done by simply watching the horizon for flying kayakers. If they can catch air, so can you.

■ It's not uncommon for the boat to land upside down—so a good roll is essential.

Pop-ups From Pourovers

Pourovers are formed when water is channeled around an obstruction in the current and then falls a short distance. Next to this chute of water and downstream of the obstruction an eddy forms. To do the pop-up, paddle forward in the eddy and punch the chute with your bow at its strongest

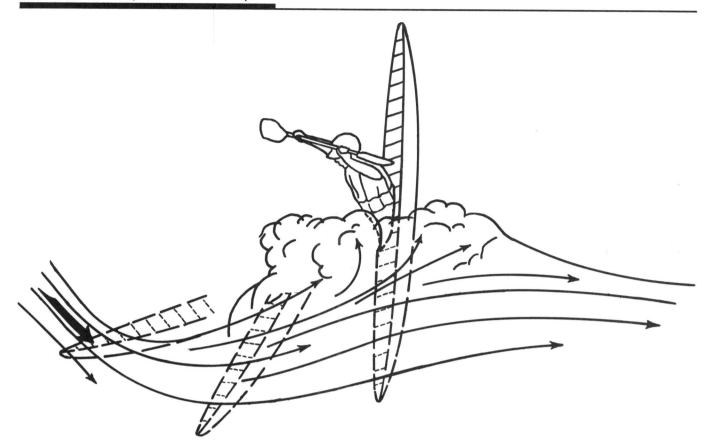

Figure 14.1: A breaking wave is a great place to do pop-ups.

point, usually right next to the rock it is pouring off of, as in figure 14.2. A churning, unstable eddy may make this considerably harder than it sounds. If your boat is not pointed directly upstream as your bow begins to pearl, shift your edges (this usually means dropping your upstream edge slightly) so the flat surface of your deck takes the full brunt of the current. Lean briskly forward at the moment of entry. Holding your forward lean will tend to cartwheel the boat; a backward lean as the bow is forced down will hold you in a more vertical position.

Occasionally, two rocks will form a strong central chute of water, and this is by far the easiest place to do pop-ups. Often no maneuvering is required; guide your bow into the chute and the water will do the rest of the job for you.

Pop-ups From Holes

When rocky obstructions are completely submerged, they tend to form hydraulics or holes behind them instead of eddies. Most pop-up holes require some maneuvering to reach a place where your bow won't

Figure 14.2: X marks the pop-up spot for this pourover.

"ground out" during deck loading (see figure 14.3). Look for this spot between the submerged rocks forming the hole, or on the outside of the hole where water is channeled around the obstruction (like an underwater pourover). Occasionally, you'll find a hole that will pull your boat upstream and slam your bow downward into a perfect pop-up without even taking a stroke.

Take care that you hold your deck perpendicular to the current and that you don't enter the hole at a significant angle, or your boat may be flipped upside down and sideways in the hole instead of being thrown free. Experiment in friendly holes, and work your way up to the adrenaline pumping stuff. When you feel comfortable playing in a hole, try stern pop-ups, also known as "back-enders."

Pop-ups From Breaking Waves

You can get beautiful pop-ups on many steep waves or those with a breaking wave crest. The trick is to control the kayak's surfing angle skillfully so you can reach the best (usually the steepest) section of wave,

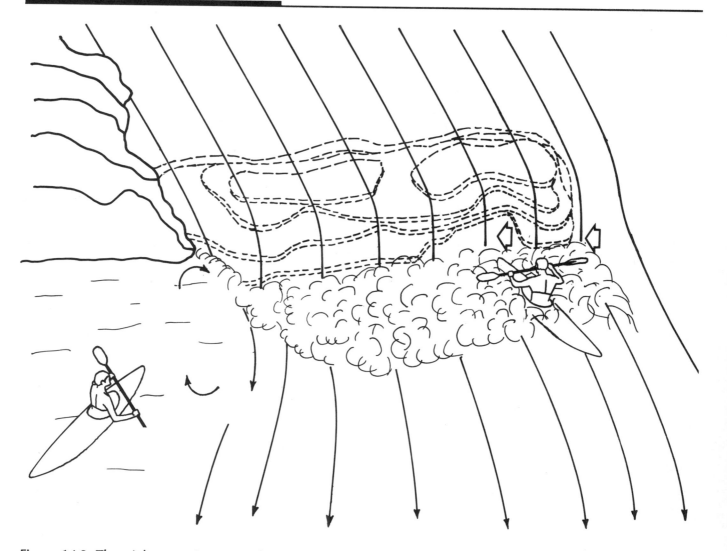

Figure 14.3: The trick to getting vertical in a hole is usually finding a spot between rocks where your bow has room to dive. The arrows show two possibilities in this hole.

and then slide straight forward into the oncoming current without catching an edge.

Begin your bow-surf with a backward lean, keeping the boat high on the wave, almost nestled in the crest. This gives you the best directional control and the opportunity to plunge the whole height of the wave into the trough for the pop-up. Drive off the top of the wave and then lean briskly forward. The trough of a wave is usually flatter than that of a hole, so the bow usually needs to be "weighted" in order to force the bow to pearl into the oncoming water.

Pirouettes

▪ There's always a good chance you'll land upside down even if you do this technique right!

When you can produce pop-ups on command, it's time to try pirouettes. A pirouette is a pop-up which corkscrews out of the water. Immediately after your bow buries itself enroute to a pop-up, create a spinning motion by either stroking strongly downward and backward on one side of the boat with a backstroke (as shown in figure 14.4 a-f), or by using a cross-bow stroke (as shown in 14.5 a, b). If you have the initial pop-up cinched, it will more than likely turn into a beautiful pirouette. If it wasn't, you will crash and burn; but try it anyway. There's always a good chance you'll land upside down even if you do this technique right!

The quicker and more natural movement is to use a backstroke, because you hold the paddle in its normal position and can use it to guide your entry into the pop-up, and help the stern rise higher into the air. You'll most often see this technique used when entering a pirouette from a bow-surf.

The cross-bow technique requires more commitment, because as your bow moves forward into the pop-up, the paddle must be held out of the water in preparation for the cross-bow stroke, and is unavailable for last minute corrections in direction or speed. A cross-bow technique probably works best at a pourover. Paddling from the eddy downstream of a pourover into the pop-up allows you to time your movements better, and to raise your blade in preparation for a well defined entry.

Using either technique, begin the pirouette while the kayak's stern is still climbing upward. Strong knee pressure as your paddle bites into current powers the spin, and a twisting motion with your upper body in the direction of the spin sustains it. Pulling your hands into the boat's side after taking your stroke will increase the kayak's spin just as it does for a ballerina or ice skater, and it will help you to set up for the inevitable roll.

With good balance, lots of practice, and driving early with the knees, you might be able to coax more than one revolution out of a well-executed pirouette, but most people get less than one. It can be completed in fine

A

Figure 14.4 a: A pirouette performed with a backstroke. When the left blade enters the water, sometime between A and B (on the following page), the current will begin to spin the kayak.

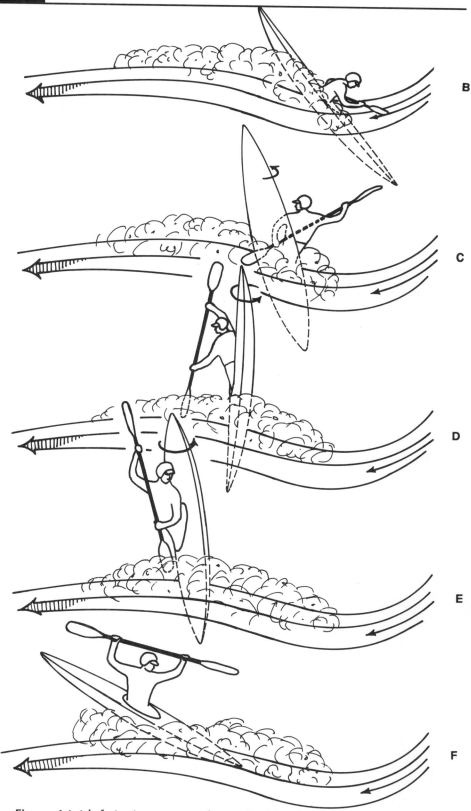

Figure 14.4 b-f: A pirouette performed with a backstroke. The backstroke occurs while the kayak is still moving upward (between C and D) and lifts the boat as well as spins it.

Figure 14.5 a: A pirouette performed with a cross-bow stroke. Although this illustration depicts a wave, the cross-bow stroke probably works better with a pourover. Prepare for the cross-bow stroke as the bow begins to pearl.

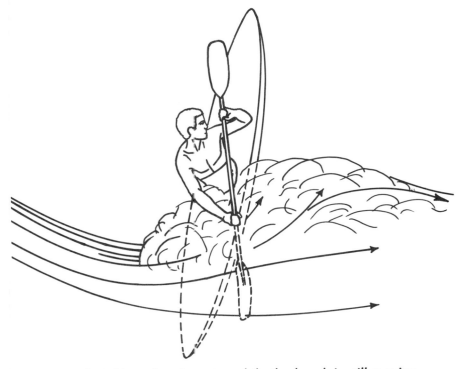

Figure 14.5 b: Initiate the pirouette while the kayak is still moving upward.

form without landing on your head by sweeping your blade across the water's surface *just before* your boat crashes back into the water, and hipsnapping the kayak upright. The pirouette is a striking acrobatic move when done well, and a lot of fun to boot.

Hole playing develops the following skills: stable side-surfing, the ability to maneuver back and forth in the hole, the ability to exit when you want to, and a hole roll. Holes come in all shapes, sizes, and temperaments. In this chapter I discuss how to play in your average friendly hole, which lacks protruding rocks, is deep enough to hold a kayak but not difficult to escape from if good technique is used, and has an eddy a mile long below it; a safe, enjoyable play-hole, a good place to learn new techniques. Hole-playing skills described here, once learned, will serve you well in mean, steep, aerated holes if you mistakenly land in one.

Side-Surfing

The single most important variable when side-surfing is whether you hold your body over the kayak, or allow it to fall or "lean" downstream into the current. One style is nearly effortless, extremely stable, and is useful in big holes and small ones, the other way is "iffy."

The kayaker in figure 15.1 a holds his upstream edge out of the current by leaning downstream. Some sculling is often necessary to maintain stability. Because his paddle adds drag, he will wash out of small holes, and have trouble moving from side to side in larger ones. When feeling insecure or tired, he may lean farther downstream to keep the upstream edge of the boat out of the current, or to try to improve the effectiveness of his brace. This may lead to the situation in figure 15.1 b.

The "upstream" edge of this kayak will definitely not catch in the current; however, the kayak is no longer giving the paddler any support. He can't look around or effectively paddle forward or backward because considerable effort is being expended just to keep his head out of the foam. A quick sculling backstroke (using the power face of the blade) is unlikely to budge the boat because of the tremendous resistance to sideways movement caused by his body in the current. The situation can easily deteriorate farther, as in figure 15.1 c. A marked downstream lean sacrifices power and control in exchange for only marginal stability while side-surfing.

The upright paddler in figure 15.2 stoutly holds the upstream edge of the kayak out of the current (despite bounce or turbulence) by a raised knee. The upright posture permits a good view of both the hole and the surrounding water. If the hole becomes "sticky," it is easy to look around

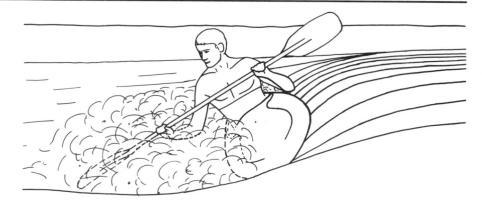

Figure 15.1 a: The average kayaker leans on the paddle somewhat while side-surfing. This adds drag and decreases your ability to slide easily back and forth in the hole.

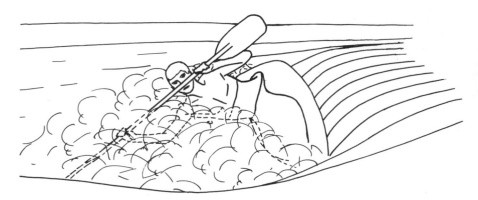

Figure 15.1 b: Leaning on a downstream brace can result in "falling" to the downstream side, and . . .

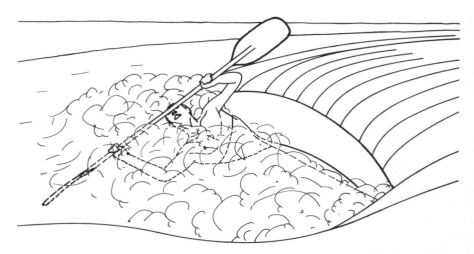

Figure 15.1 c: . . . as we saw with regard to paddle rolls, lifting your head upward when your body is unsupported by the kayak can result in pulling the boat upside down.

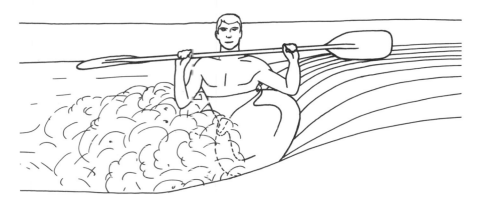

Figure 15.2 This paddler stoutly holds the upstream edge of the kayak out of the current and keeps his weight over the boat by sitting up-right.

for a way out. Since the kayak alone supports this paddler's weight, he uses much less energy to stay upright. The paddle exerts no drag whatsoever, and is used mostly for balance, and now and then for a brief brace. Paddle twirling is an excellent test of this paddler's balance and control. Most friendly holes can be side-surfed in just this way.

Another advantage of an upright posture is your ability to carefully decrease the steepness of your edge tilt in certain situations. A large edge tilt will "bite" into the current, significantly increase drag, and cause the kayak to move higher up on the pillow, bounce, or break out of the side-surf. This is especially true in small holes with little holding power, and when side-surfing a breaking wave (a breaking wave is almost a hole, but

Figure 15.3: Decreasing your edge tilt slightly will occasionally stabilize or smooth out your surf by allowing the kayak to slide back into the hole. The reduction in drag will help you stay in some holes you might otherwise wash out of.

most of the water is blasting right through the "hole" without recirculating). Decreasing your edge tilt slightly (being careful not to catch your upstream edge) will often allow the kayak to "slide" back toward the trough, as shown in figure 15.3.

The Dangers of an Overhead Brace

There is an unfortunate belief among many beginning paddlers that a high brace using an overhead hand position is a useful technique to help them side-surf and back out of holes, especially large holes with a large pillow. At first most paddlers are intimidated by large holes, and their instincts are to lean downstream away from them and reach over the pillow to brace. This is not only poor technique, it is dangerous. AN OVERHEAD HAND POSITION DURING *ANY* HIGH BRACE INCREASES YOUR RISK FOR SHOULDER DISLOCATION !!

The shoulder is the most mobile joint in the body. It is strongest when your arm is flexed and your hand is in front of your chest, the position you would assume when boxing or arm wrestling. It is weakest and least stable when your arm is raised, and your hand and elbow are held behind your head. Violent whitewater can force either hand backward during an overhead brace, and dislocate a shoulder. This commonly occurs when a side-surfing kayaker tries to scull his way backward out of a hole and catches an edge, as in figure 15.4. The kayak can be powerfully rolled upstream, dragging and swinging the torso behind it. Injury is almost certain if the upstream blade strikes a rock.

■ Violent whitewater can force either hand backward during an overhead brace, and dislocate a shoulder.

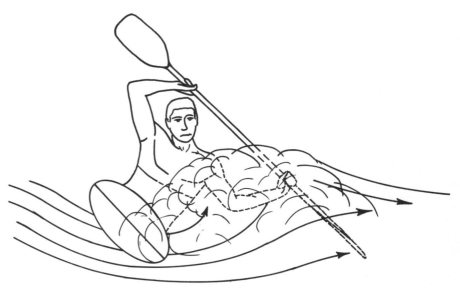

Figure 15.4 a: An overhead brace is especially risky while side-surfing. See also figure 15.4 b-c.

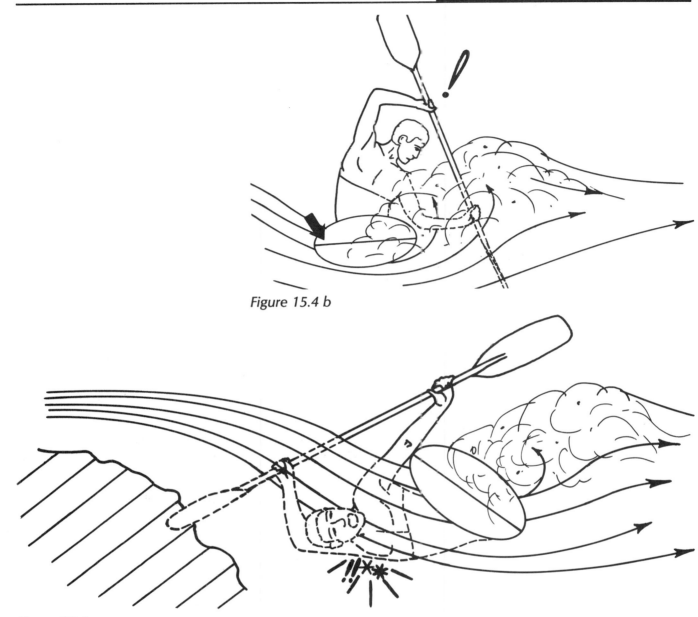

Figure 15.4 b

Figure 15.4 c

Many paddlers continue to use an overhead brace position in spite of its shortcomings, which is the reason shoulder dislocations remain the most common serious kayaking injury.

This is a problem of technique, not conditioning. The strongest, most effective brace stroke occurs when both arms are flexed and both hands held near the chest, like figure 15.2. This is true even if you're side-surfing a pillow higher than your head—brace into the pillow. You don't need to reach over it (figure 15.5). The inboard hand, held below your forehead and near your chest, protects your shoulders by making your chest a block to any backward motion of the paddle shaft. Never brace with an overhead hand position!

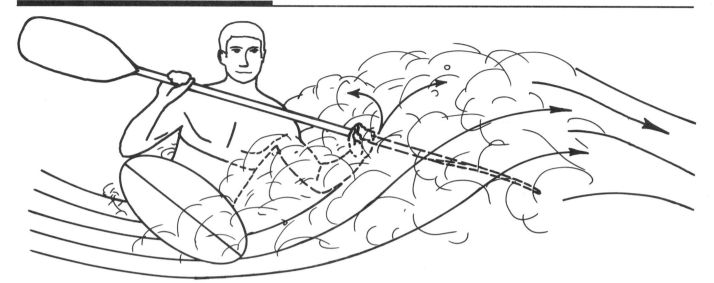

Figure 15.5: This should generally be your high brace position while side-surfing.

Continuous Bracing

When the upstream "wall" of the hole becomes steep, you will need an exaggerated edge tilt for stability. In this situation, use some sort of sustained brace stroke to maintain your balance. I feel a bread-and-butter stroke (linked together sweep brace strokes) has significant advantages over a sculling stroke. The sculling paddler uses only the power face of the blade in a back and forth fanning motion. He must side-surf with his body close to or partially in the water because a backstroke using the power face of the blade requires considerable wrist extension and a back lean. The bread-and-butter stroke alternates using the blade's power face (for a forward sweep brace) and the blade's back face (for a back sweep brace). Use of this stroke permits you to sit upright, head well out of the water, during your side-surf. Because no part of your arm or body drags in the current, the boat remains slippery, and it is easy to slide back and forth from one side of the hole to the other.

To move the boat forward, replace the paired sweep brace strokes with a regular forward stroke alternating with a back sweep brace. Move the kayak backward with a powerful back stroke, alternating with a forward sweep brace. This backstroke is far more powerful than any sculling backstroke because both shoulders and the trunk (not just the hands and arms) give it power. Improve balance by using the sweep brace in one direction, while supplying power by using the industrial strength standard stroke in the other direction. The bread-and-butter stroke dramatically improves your ability to play in holes, and keeps your arms safely down to protect your shoulders.

What about bracing on the upstream side of a hole when you catch your edge? It's widely acknowledged that this is an unsafe thing to do, and rolling is better than trying to free a buried edge and risking injury to your shoulders. This is often true, but sometimes it's not, depending upon the power of the hole, as well as your training and skill. What's indisputable is that people instinctively do upstream bracing all the time in playboating situations. In this setting, a fast sweeping bread-and-butter stroke is far safer and more effective than any high brace, low brace, or sculling stroke.

Diagonal-Surfing

Diagonal-surfing is my term for remaining in one place while surfing a wave or hole with your boat at an angle to the current. Actually, it's hard to classify a place where you can diagonal surf as either a hole or a wave, it's often not a place you see as much as feel. Think of it as surfing a wave trough and crest that are aligned at an angle to the current, instead of perpendicular to it, as in figure 15.6. If you try to bow-surf or side-surf, you'll end up either sliding upstream until your bow pearls in the trough and pushes your boat over the downstream pillow, or, if you apply increased back pressure with your downstream blade to prevent sliding forward, you'll turn the boat sideways to the current, and pearl the bow or slide backward off the pillow. A momentary surf is all many paddlers can manage. They don't realize that they can diagonally surf that spot using an upstream rudder/backstroke and hold the kayak in one stable place on the wave.

These surfing opportunities occur all the time on the river. For instance, you can surf in the downstream angled trough next to some pourovers, on diagonal waves, and sometimes in the hydraulic behind ledges if the current forms intermittent pillows. In most cases, the kayak sits on an inclined plane with its bow in some kind of trough or depression (as it would bow-surfing a wave), and rests against a downstream pillow (as it would side-surfing a hole). This is a balancing act—moving forward throws the bow downstream, moving back slides you off the pillow.

While surfing the current at an angle, your task is to keep your bow pointing upstream and your stern high enough on the pillow to permit you to surf down its face. You can only do this by holding your kayak firmly on edge for stability, and by applying a strong, sustained upstream rudder. Almost continuous back pressure on the paddle is necessary, or your boat will turn sideways to the current and be blown downstream. Adding or decreasing drag with your rudder keeps the boat from moving too far forward or backward. It requires good balance and edge control to reach

▪ This is a balancing act—moving forward throws the bow downstream, moving back slides you off the pillow.

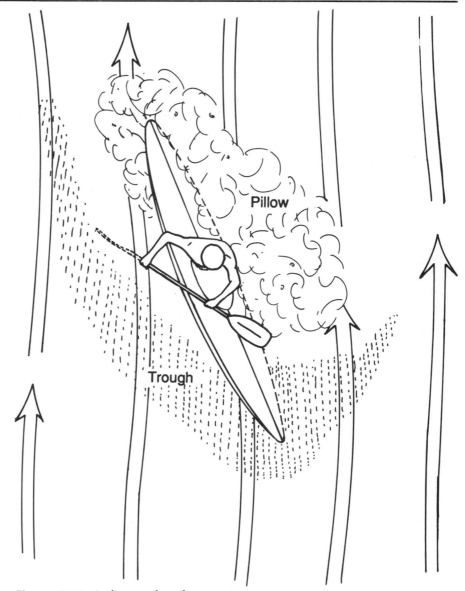

Figure 15.6: A diagonal surf.

over the upper rail of the kayak and firmly plant your upstream blade in the river. You may feel nervous the first couple of times you try it, but persevere (and don't lean on your paddle). It works.

The Hole Roll (or "Window Shade" Maneuver)

The hole roll is an upstream roll performed while side-surfing. This is strictly a playboating technique, done with the intention of continuing the side-surf and remaining in the hole following the roll. Only attempt this maneuver if you have plenty of water under the upstream side of your boat. If you can see the rock forming the hole you are in, don't try it!

Begin the hole roll in the setup position, but with your paddle on top of the deck rather than over the side. This will keep your hands and wrists from being wrenched if the current catches your paddle before it flips the kayak. Take a deep breath, lean upstream, and keep your head near the deck of the kayak or you risk getting knocked silly! As current hits the boat's upstream edge, you'll be suddenly flipped upside down.

You'll find that in some holes your kayak seems so stable that tipping the boat upstream is surprisingly difficult. This occurs because as you attempt to lower the upstream edge by lowering your knee, you are, in essence, sitting upright. To avoid sitting upright, you remain tucked forward and the kayak stubbornly stays right where it is, in a stable side-surf. The best way to encourage your boat to flip is not to relax your upstream knee, but to gently "throw" yourself from an upright posture into a tight tucked forward setup position. Allow your momentum to tip the kayak off balance while your head remains safely against the deck.

▪ Allow your momentum to tip the kayak off balance while your head remains safely against the deck.

After the boat flips, gently sweep your paddle to the side, and allow the current to "blow" it downstream. Don't worry about sweeping toward the surface, because the whole force of the current is already pushing your paddle in that direction. Slow hip rotation will bring you back into a stable side-surf with good edge control and your weight balanced over the boat. Caution is advised: a too-vigorous hipsnap could result in a violent upstream corkscrew roll, so fast you won't know what happened. If you are sitting upright when this occurs, your head may be swung into an upstream rock! Do not allow your upstream edge to catch in the current during your hipsnap; the kayak will assume a stable side-surf long before you rotate its edges "level."

Timing your roll is often important in smaller holes where your kayak won't remain centered in the lowest part of the hole for more than a moment or two. It may oscillate back and forth from one side of the hole to the other, being pushed by the current "uphill" toward a corner, or sliding "downhill" toward the center. Time your roll so that your momentum carries you toward the hole's center. A window shade creates a lot of drag as your body enters the current, so that if you roll when your boat is being pushed toward a corner, close to the "rim" of the hole, you are more likely to be blown out during the roll.

Window shading, when done in a safe hole and with good technique, is a blast. After you get used to the technique, you'll find it's as easy to do without a paddle as with one. Try holding your paddle in reserve, cradled under your upstream arm, as in figure 15.7 a. The current will blow your paddle downstream during your roll. Allow it to unwind away from your body and into the air as you reach out to the side with your free hand, as shown in figure 15.7 b. The current should push you right to the surface—it does 98 percent of the work during this roll. Use your hand

Figure 15.7 a: One-hand window shade maneuver holding your paddle in reserve. A The setup position just before the roll. Hold the paddle tightly under your arm. If you allow the current to grab it before the kayak rolls upside down, the paddle will be violently wrenched from your hand.

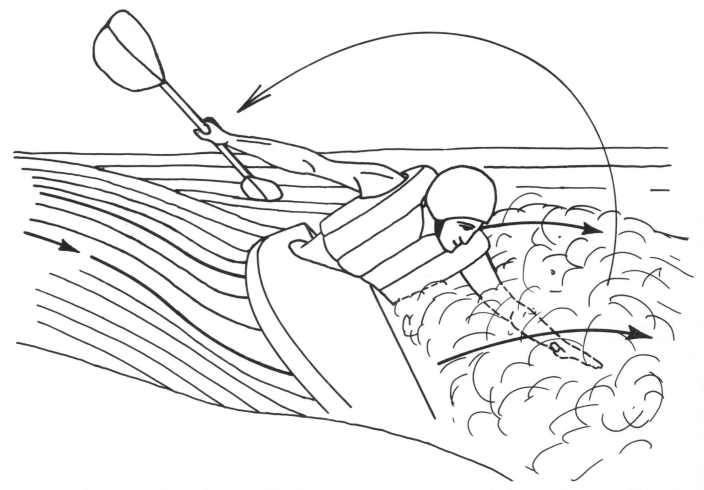

Figure 15.7 b: As you roll upright, assisted by the current, continue to rotate the boat's edges smoothly until your head is again over the deck, your weight supported by the kayak.

and arm to brace, and rotate the kayak back under your body using knee pressure. To move your head back over your boat, it might also help to lean forward and bring your bracing hand in next to the rail. Whatever you do, don't lean away from the boat and onto your hand, it won't support you! Regrip your paddle whenever you want to.

360-Degree Turns

■ Even in well-formed holes there is always continuous maneuvering required to attain or maintain good position.

One of the best ways to fine-tune all your river playing skills is to do 360-degree turns in a gentle hole. A 360 can be initiated from either a bow- or stern-surfing position on the crest of the hole, or from a side-surf. The idea is to move your kayak onto the crest of the hole at one corner where it can spin easily, a place we'll call the "sweet spot." A sweet spot usually exists if the ends of both your bow and stern are out of the water when surfing the recirculating foamy white pillow of the hole's crest, and where there is good contrast between this "white" water and the dark downstream current, or "greenwater," flowing past the outside of the hole. The greenwater is used to assist each "pivot turn" on the pillow by forcing one end of the kayak downstream. An aerial view of such a play spot is diagrammed in figure 15.8 (this is my depiction of the near corner of the hole shown in figure 15.11 a).

Unfortunately, talk of spinning your kayak through 360-degree turns while pivoting about the sweet spot vastly oversimplifies this maneuver. Even in well-formed holes there is always continuous maneuvering required to attain or maintain good position. First let's talk about edge control, and the paddle strokes needed to maneuver with stability during 360s, and then let's review the special case where you do attain the sweet spot and can spin on it. There are, of course, many approaches to playboating, and the techniques I describe are only suggestions.

Figures 15.9 a and b illustrate a full 360 degree turn. Use the two figures together to mentally "walk through" the entire maneuver. If you were to begin your first turn from a bow-surfing position review each of the eight steps beginning from #8, then 1, 2, 3, 4, 5, 6, 7, 8, 1, etc. To begin by paddling forward from a side-surfing position begin at #2, then 3, 4, 5, 6, 7, 8, 1, 2, etc. My description will begin at #6 (as if beginning the 360 by paddling backward from a side-surfing position) because you are looking upstream toward the hole during the first four steps. Paddle stokes during the more difficult second half of the 360, the blind half, will then be easier to understand. As you follow the text closely, look at the appropriate illustration.

Initiate the 360 by backstroking out the side of the hole, as shown in figure 15.9 b, boat position #6. You'll need to power the kayak far enough into greenwater so that it strongly pushes your stern downstream and forces the entire kayak upward onto the pillow. Immediately place a rudder stroke into greenwater next to the stern, before your boat attains its bow-surfing position (figure 15.9 b, position #7). This rudder stroke makes use of water flowing past or through the hole to keep the kayak

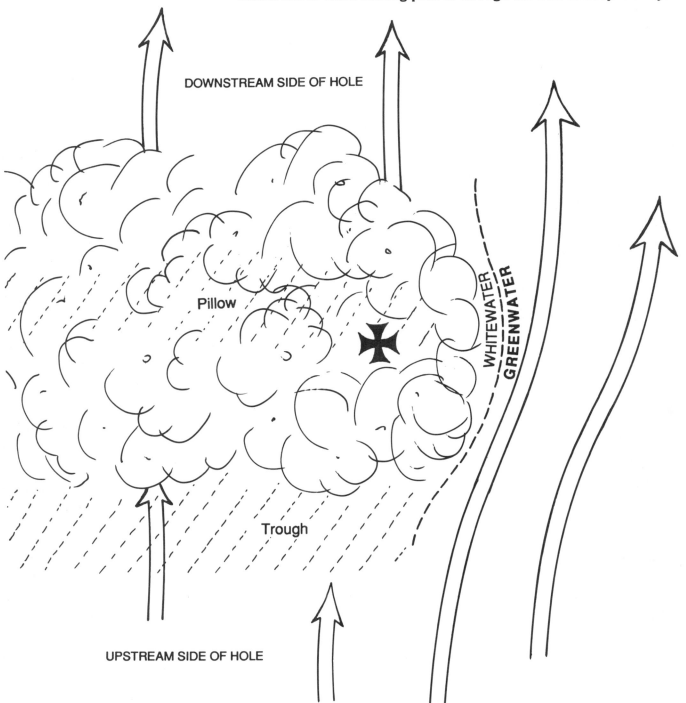

DOWNSTREAM SIDE OF HOLE

Pillow

WHITEWATER

GREENWATER

Trough

UPSTREAM SIDE OF HOLE

Figure 15.8: Diagram of a 360 hole. The dashed greenwater/whitewater line shows where the aerated recirculating water of the hole is rimmed by the dark unaerated downstream flowing water just to the outside of the hole. The X is the hole's "sweet spot," an imaginery point on the pillow near the corner of the hole on which, or around which, the kayak can do 360s.

from sliding upstream into the trough; it also pushes your stern away from greenwater and through your first pivot turn and edge shift (figure 15.9 b, position #8). This is an intuitive action to many because both the bow and the hole's trough are in plain view, and the needed technique is identical to that used to change the direction of a bow-surf (indeed, this is all you are doing).

As the boat approaches a bow-surf, smoothly, confidently, shift your edges and allow the kayak to slide, bow first, back into the hole in the same direction from which it left. The boat's momentum as it slides into the hole will help propel it partially out the side into greenwater again. Your downstream blade controls your hole speed (figure 15.9 a, position #1), and your position relative to the greenwater/whitewater line (figure 15.9 a, position #2). At this point a forward stroke moves the boat further into greenwater and higher onto the crest (or clean past the crest if your forward speed is too great); back pressure on your paddle slows the boat (too much back pressure might leave you in the trough, side-surfing). If your control is just right, the boat's bow and stern feel weightless and effortless to spin as your kayak rises back onto the pillow.

Your next move is the critical one, a blind pivot turn with your back toward the hole. You can't see your stern's relationship to the hole's trough, so if you're not firmly in control, your edge shift will be indecisive as you wait to find out whether the boat will swing all the way through the turn. A slow pivot turn or indecision during this momentary stern-surf can result in a back ender as the boat slides straight upstream and pearls, or result in a windowshade because you've allowed an upstream edge to catch.

The best technique is one analogous to that used in the first half of the turn. Take your downstream blade out of the water, and place your upstream blade in greenwater next to the bow before your boat aligns with the current (figure 15.9 a, position #3). This "bow-rudder" functions the same as the stern rudder in the first half of the 360: it prevents the stern from sliding forward and pearling in the trough, it helps hold the kayak up on the pillow, and it uses the current to push the kayak through the pivot turn and edge shift (15.9 a, position #4). Initiating your next turn is simply a matter of allowing the momentum you gain sliding back into the hole to help propel your kayak partially out the side into greenwater (15.9 b, position #5).

The often neglected key to the blind half of the turn is the bow-rudder stroke. Many paddlers apply it late or neglect it entirely because it is an upstream stroke performed without seeing your stern's relationship to the hole's trough. Alternate ways of encouraging the pivot turn (like pushing the downstream blade in 15.9 a, position #2 strongly toward the bow) generally don't allow the same definite shifting of your edges as a bow-rudder.

Weight shifting, forward or aft, is sometimes crucial in 360s where much of the action takes place on the crest of the hole. A simple weight shift can make the difference between being blown downstream, or sliding back into the hole. Make these fore and aft leans momentary,

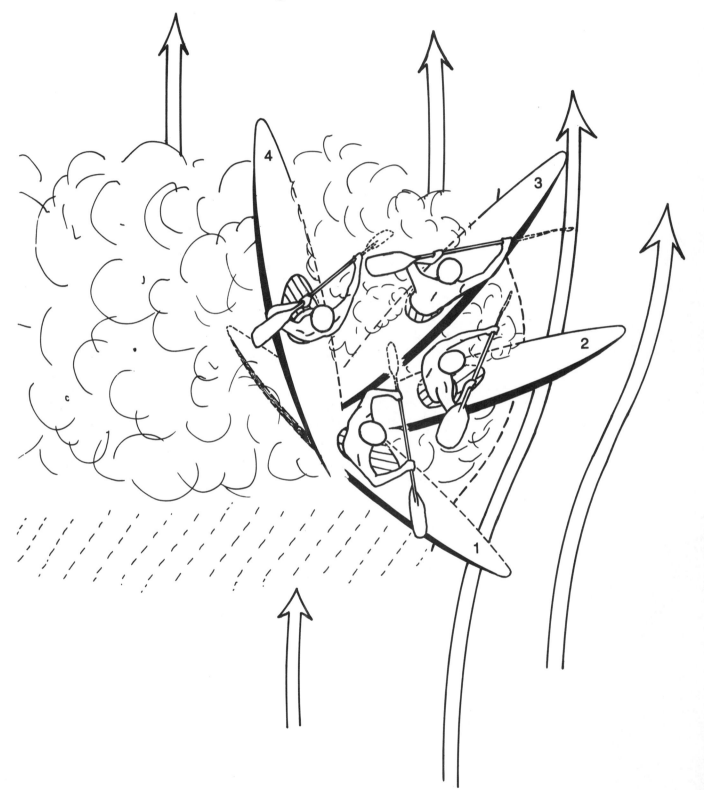

Figure 15.9 a: The first half of a 360.

though so that you don't pearl the stern or bow when sliding back toward the hole's trough, and so that your weight is back over the center of the boat when you have to do your next pivot turn. If your weight is off-center or you lean on your paddle blade, the kayak doesn't spin as easily and good edge control becomes difficult. You'll rarely need weight shifts,

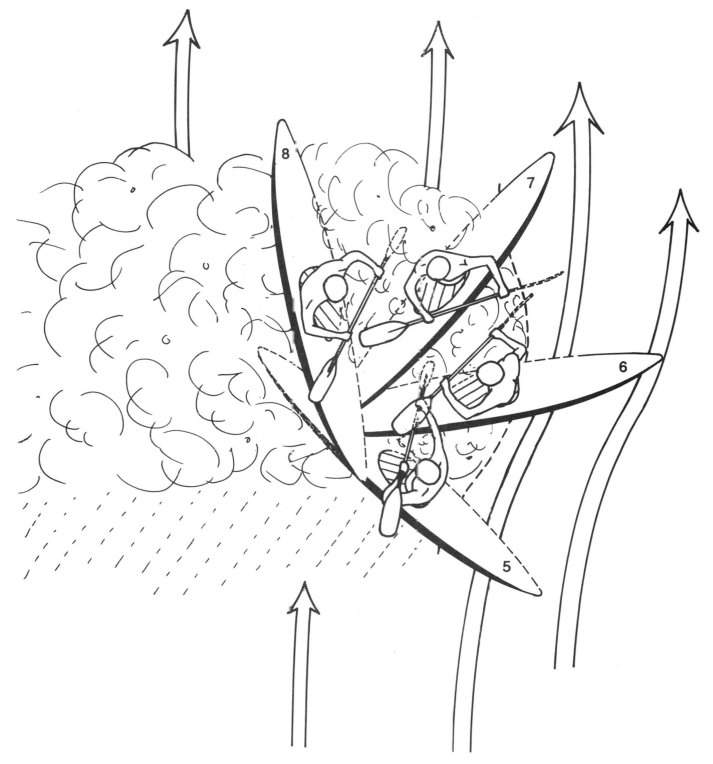

Figure 15.9 b: The second half of a 360.

however, if forward or back paddle pressure in positions #1 and #5 controls your momentum, and moves your boat into good position on the pillow.

In the purest form, successive 360s require only one switch in blade from downstream to upstream side before each edge shift, linking one

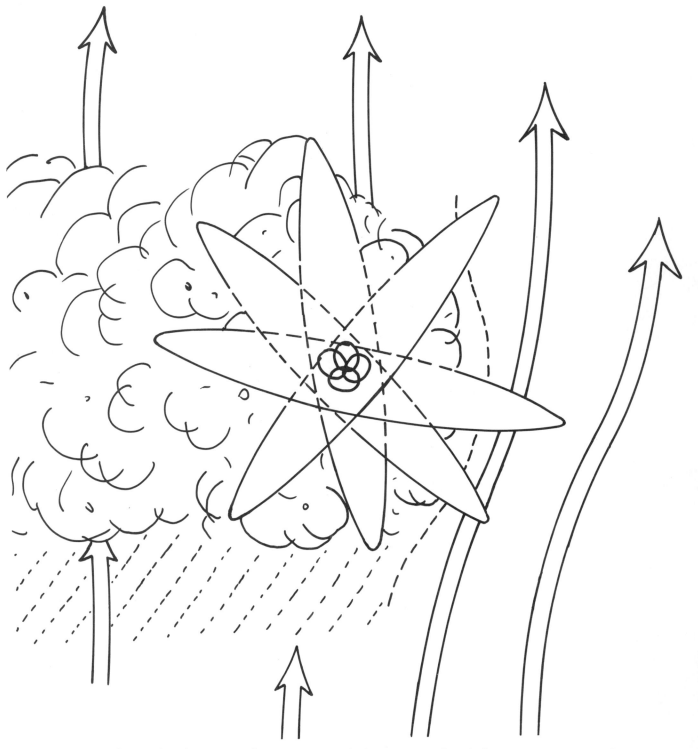

Figure 15.9 c: With good technique and a cooperative hole you can often link succesive turns without moving your head more than a foot or two.

turn to another rhythmically. Deft paddle strokes keep your boat's spinning motion in the corner of the hole uninterrupted, and because your pivot turns are under control, edge shifts are confident and well-timed. With practice, you'll reduce the magnitude of the large motions I've described here, which move your kayak from the hole's trough to its crest, back and forth. Large edge tilts, hard strokes, and big leans will become unnecessary. You'll begin to link your turns and spin the kayak while surfing the pillow, astride the sweet spot, without having to resort to sliding back into the trough to power your turns (figure 15.9 c).

A significant change in the way you control your edges can, and should, occur when you begin to link your turns in this way: hold your edges absolutely flat. A pivot turn completed on top of the pillow with flat edges will maintain stability because the entire upstream rail will be out of the water at every point of the turn. In fact, repeated turns in the sweet spot require almost flat edges to prevent the kayak from inadvertently carving into the current, and to make it easy to spin the boat quickly by keeping your weight smack over the pivot point of each turn. Exceptional technique and flat edges allow a highly skilled paddler to do pivot turns on many poorly defined pillows and even some breaking waves. In these marginal situations the kayak will be forced off the pillow and downstream if there is any hesitation during a turn or unnecessary drag, as can be caused by large edge tilts.

360s are a fun challenge and a real measure of boating skill. Every hole is unique, and will require you to adjust your technique to cater to that hole's peculiarities. Your bow-surfing and side-surfing skills will be taxed. Initially, you'll use many extraneous paddle strokes to control the boat, but in time your kayak will need much less encouragement. Make the current do most of the work for you, and turning 360s will become a supervisory job, not heavy manual labor.

The Polish Maneuver

One advantage of turning consistent 360s is that it gives you the opportunity to guide the kayak upstream into an aerial maneuver like a Polish each time you unload the bow and stern on the hole's crest. A Polish maneuver can be considered a hybrid between a window shade and a pirouette. The kayak is rolled in the hole, but in such a way that one end of the boat clearly moves through the air (the stern catches air if the Polish is entered from a bow-surf). You'll need a hole stable enough for side-surfing, but deep enough for pop-ups to pull off this difficult move.

Begin the Polish by guiding your kayak upstream as if to do a pop-

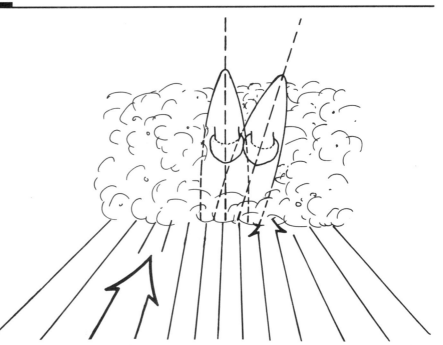

Figure 15.10: The entrance into a Polish differs from that of a pirouette in that the kayak enters the maneuver at a slight angle to the current.

up, but drop into the trough at a slight angle to the current, as in figure 15.10. Dropping in at an angle will pearl your upstream edge and begin to roll the kayak's stern over your back as it rises into an off-angle, pop-up position. The ends of the boat will pivot around its cockpit: as the bow moves downstream with the current, the stern will rise out of the water and swing upstream, cartwheeling the boat stern over bow. This leaves you upstream of the pillow with the opportunity to guide the kayak

Figure 15.11 a: The Polish maneuver. Although it's difficult to appreciate from this vantage point, the kayak is sliding towards the trough angled to the paddler's right. As the bow pearls, the stern will rise and swing toward the viewer.

Figure 15.11 b: Lean forward over the trough as the bow begins to pearl.

Figure 15.11 c: Keep your head up as you twist your body and swing your paddle downstream.

backward into a side-surf using a strong backstroke.

The trick to completing the Polish is to complement the kayak's pop–up/rolling motion with a turning/twisting movement of your upper body, which I've tried to illustrate in figures 15.11 a through e. As you enter the Polish from a bow-surf (figure 15.11 a), lean upstream as the bow pearls, as shown in figure 15.11 b. This will help lift the stern and pearl the bow, as well as help keep your weight upstream of the pillow. When your kayak approaches the pop-up position and you begin to feel your weight shift onto the foot braces, turn your head, upper body, and

Figure 15.11 d: The kayak will follow your body's lead and rotate onto its right tail.

Figure 15.11 e: Backstroke to finish boat rotation (so that your weight is again supported by the kayak), and to move the kayak back toward the trough.

shoulders strongly downstream (figure 15.11 c). Rick Williams, winner of the 1988 Wenachee River Rodeo in Washington, describes this as throwing the stern of your boat over your back like a sack of potatoes. Swing your paddle in front of you as the stern rises and moves overhead. As you twist around, the kayak will roll onto its side and the stern will land in the water near the trough (figure 15.11 d). Your trailing blade provides a large backstroke that helps to slide the kayak fully back into the hole (figure 15.11 e). You enter the maneuver bow-surfing and finish it side-surfing.

A well-executed Polish will loft one end of your kayak well out of the water and give you plenty of room to twist downstream under the boat.

Keep your head up as the kayak pivots completely around your body (as shown in the illustration), and your hair won't even get wet. Not infrequently, however, you won't catch as much air as you'd like and your technique will resemble a window shade in form more than a Polish; your body and paddle will move (to a greater or lesser degree) into the pillow instead of over it.

The Polish is popular in whitewater rodeo competitions where contestants try to do as many hole-playing tricks as possible during one ride or within a specified time limit. Aerials like pop-ups and pirouettes are usually attempted only in the final seconds of a round because they almost always result in a hole exit and lost time. The Polish maneuver leaves the kayak in a side-surf ready to do the next move, which might be a window shade, entry into a 360, or a 360 linked to another Polish. Polishes can be done with a stern entry, and like window shades and 360s, they can be linked together or done without a paddle.

Playboating in a friendly river hydraulic on a hot summer's day just about tops the list of my favorite things to do. When river running, I see what maneuvers I can extract out of almost every wave and hole I come across. This enthusiasm sometimes leads me to drop into places where I really didn't want to be and getting out then becomes the most important hole playing skill. . .

When you get that sinking feeling that you don't have the hole, but that it has you, don't panic. Solidly support the boat's upstream edge with your knee and try to get stable in the hole. Sit upright and look around; plan what you'll do next. If the hole is very steep or violent, you may not have this luxury. Regardless, you generally must choose among the following options in decreasing order of preference: 1. Paddle out of the hole right-side-up, 2. Escape from the hole upside-down, 3. Pull off your spray skirt so the boat fills with water, becomes less buoyant, and washes out underneath the hole, and 4. Swim. I have never tried option 3 intentionally, although I have had my sprayskirt torn off in violent holes, and my boat and I washed out quite nicely after that. I have considerable experience with options 1 and 2 which I've outlined below; these suggestions should help make swimming a rare occurrence.

The first maneuver you should try is to paddle forward or backward out the hole's side with a bread-and-butter stroke. Moving the kayak strongly to either side of the hole gives you many escape options even if the kayak fails to reach hole escape velocity with your first effort. If the boat slows and then stops on the hole's perimeter, you can powerfully stroke back into the hole, across it, and out the opposite side.

One way to increase the power of your back-and-forth movements, especially near the corners of a hole, is to take paddle strokes on both sides of the kayak. This is an advanced skill. You must use a large climbing blade angle on each upstream stroke to keep the paddle from catching in the current and diving. The faster the downstream current, the more brisk the upstream forward or back stroke must be near the center of the hole where the paddle sweeps directly across the current. Near the corners, the kayak usually angles downstream somewhat, your upstream blade becomes more perpendicular to the strong currents flowing around the outside of the hole, and a more sustained stroke can be used.

Newcomers to upstream paddle strokes should first try an upstream forward stroke in a gentle hole, using less than full power to develop balance and blade control. It may take several tries to get the upstream blade to work for you, but with practice you'll develop confidence in it. It's most useful when judiciously applied in sticky, small to medium sized holes. It shouldn't be used in really big holes with a wide trough where you can't reach upstream water with your paddle, or steep holes where you have to use a brace stroke to maintain balance.

During most escape maneuvers, use your paddle to move the kayak one way or the other in the hole, while you use edge control to maintain stability and use lean to keep your weight mostly over the kayak and off your paddle. This is a good rule of thumb that allows you to take powerful strokes on either side of the kayak with security. The consequences of leaning on an upstream blade are obvious; the consequences of leaning on your downstream blade are less so. If you lean downstream, relying on the support your paddle offers to remain upright, then you may "fall" downstream when the kayak changes position in the hole and the effectiveness of your brace stroke decreases.

This is the most common mistake I see during hole escapes: leaning on a downstream draw stroke near the bow (usually while sculling) in the hope of using the strong current flowing under the hole to pull the kayak out. What often happens is that the boat grudgingly slides to the corner of the hole and angles downstream. As the current begins to flow more parallel to the kayak, it no longer helps support the boat's downstream edge (as it does while side-surfing), and the draw stroke no longer supports a lean away from the boat (figure 16.1 a). The paddle can't function well as a brace stroke, and simultaneously pull directly against current flowing parallel to the kayak. With your weight unsupported by either the kayak or your paddle, you'll roll slowly upside-down into the hole. The draw stroke finally serves only to hold the boat on the hole's periphery in an upside down stern-surf.

A sustained downstream draw stroke does work well to escape

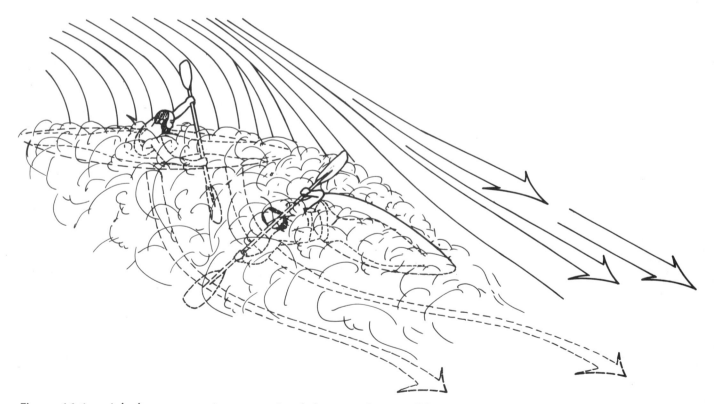

Figure 16.1 a: A hole escape using a sustained draw stroke. You'll be more successful if you keep your weight off your paddle and over your boat. This is the wrong way.

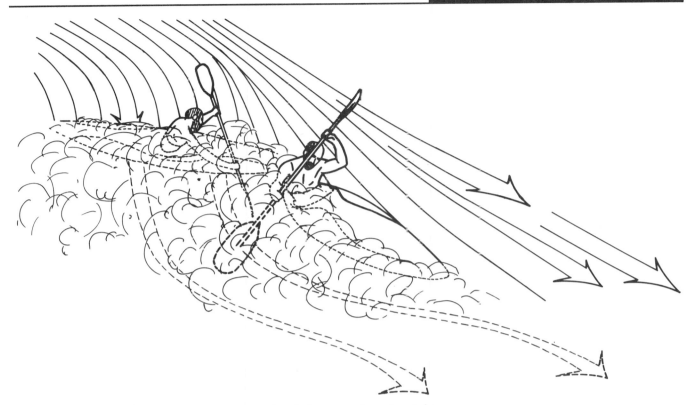

Figure 16.1 b: A hole escape using a sustained draw stroke—the right way.

many holes, but let the boat, not your paddle, support your weight, as shown in figure 16.1 b. If you can't get out of the hole on your first attempt, you'll still be upright and will have kept all your other options open.

One of these options is to paddle backward and hold a sustained backstroke on the outside perimeter of the hole in order to pivot the kayak momentarily into a bow-surfing position on the hole's crest. With locked elbows and good shoulder rotation, you can support this backstroke with your entire trunk rather than just your arms, giving it tremendous power. If you succeed in unloading your bow, you can then choose to paddle back down the wave face and across the hole, straight forward into a pop-up (this would be an act of faith; if you believe you can exit the hole by doing a pop-up, maybe you can—but don't bet on it), or punch out the near side of the hole in a powerful peel-out exit.

Punching the near side is probably your best choice. Greenwater flowing past the hole will push your bow downstream and either throw you free, or pivot the kayak 180 degrees. If the kayak pivots on the greenwater/whitewater line, once or several times, reach into the greenwater with your paddle and pull yourself strongly downstream each time. You can pinwheel downstream along the hole's perimeter using a forward stroke during the first turn, a backstroke for the second, etc. Edge control here is tricky, but no different from doing 360s under friendlier

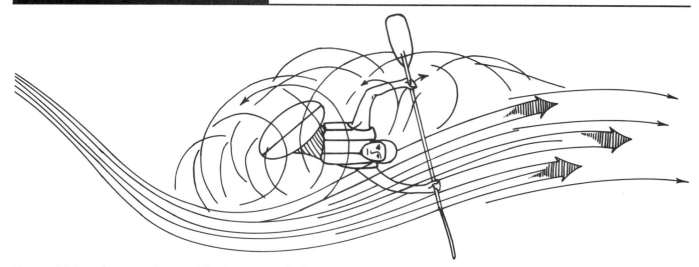

Figure 16.2: When you're upside down in a hole and trying to escape, extend both arms away from the boat to produce the greatest possible resistence to downstream current with your paddle. If you hold your anchor hand to your chest, as you would to roll, you're unlikely to create enough drag to wash out of big holes.

circumstances; only now you work yourself to the outside of the hole with each turn instead of keeping yourself on the inside.

If you can't exit the hole right-side-up, you are probably about to experiment with an upside-down exit—an excellent strategy. Although simply rolling upside down will be enough to free you from many holes, really gnarly ones often require a different technique than that used for a hole roll. After flipping over in the hole (intentionally or not), extend your body and your paddle away from the boat. Move your anchor hand well away from your chest so that you assume a position like hanging from a pull up bar, as shown in figure 16.2. One or the other of your paddle blades will be blown downstream while your kayak is held captive in the hole. Whichever blade "catches," turn it to create the greatest possible resistance to current, and hang on. When all pressure on the paddle subsides, you will more than likely be free of the hole and can set up and roll upright.

Another good last ditch strategy is to combine a side exit with a roll exit, as in figure 16.3. Paddle as far as you can to one side and then roll upside-down away from the hole, allowing your paddle and body to engage the downstream current fully. This will give you a better chance of escaping than a roll exit done in the center of the hole. Leaning to the inside is not nearly as good, because the surface water here is flowing toward the hole.

■ The best way to handle nasty, sticky, grabby, and violent holes is to avoid them.

Of course, the best way to handle nasty, sticky, grabby, and violent holes is to avoid them. Although fate sometimes deals you a bad hand, I've been lured into several holes that I should have, and could have, stayed well clear of. So before jumping into a hole, carefully assess its character and plan how you'll get out. Look at how deep the hole's trough

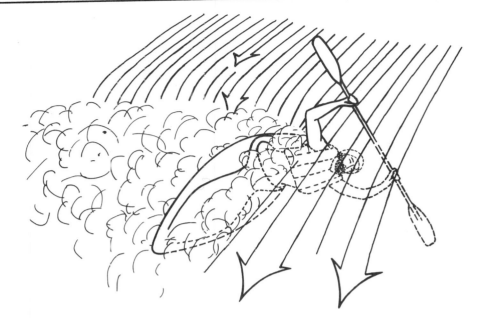

Figure 16.3: If you're foiled in your attempts to exit a hole upright, paddle as far to one side as you can and try rolling into the powerful downstream current on the outside of the hole. Get as much of your paddle and chest to engage the current as possible.

is compared to the height of its downstream pillow and corners. It will be much easier to pull yourself up and over a one foot wall of water than up and over a three-foot wall. A hole with sides "smiling" upstream will usually be harder to escape out of the corners than one smiling downstream. The corners of the upstream smiling hole may be dead-ends, ending in a rock ledge or a high wall of water, where the corners of a downstream smiling hole (much more common) are often shallow ramps leading toward the outside of the hole.

No matter how small the hole, if the upstream wall of the trough is steep, watch out! This hole will force you onto your side to keep your upstream edge free of the current. Since you can't sit upright in this situation, use a sustained paddle brace to support your side lean away from the boat, which takes a lot of work; and if the downstream pillow is deep and foamy, it will offer little paddle support and make breathing difficult—a decidedly unfriendly situation. Holes with steep upstream walls should be avoided.

Also pay careful attention to the place in the foamy pillow down-stream of the trough where foam begins to flow downstream. A hole with a large amount of water recirculating back toward the trough (say, 10 or 20 feet) may be difficult or impossible to escape from using any maneuver, sort of like paddling your way out of a continually flushing giant toilet. Any hole with significant recirculation should be considered a river hazard and should be avoided.

Look for any surging or instability in the walls of the hole. If the

■ Holes with steep upstream walls should be avoided.

downstream wall regularly breaks and flushes foam through, even large intimidating holes will be much less likely to hold your boat. A large hole with an unchanging static appearance is usually harder to break out of.

There is no all-inclusive way to exit holes. The hole escape expert moves his boat strongly back and forth in the hole and capitalizes on surges, bounce, and rocking to create instability where none existed. The boat glides and swings from side to side. A momentary catch or grab that moves the boat is accentuated by a complementary lean or paddle stroke. When escaping from holes, use all the skills you know and combine them. Add drag and body lean, then remove them. Drive forward, then reverse your drive. Create your own opportunities. Magnify each oscillation until the paddle and kayak's resistance to downstream current exceeds gravity's hold, and you break out of the hole. This activity should not be frantic, but paced and controlled. Sticky, grabby holes are rarely overpowered, they are outsmarted. A smart, skilled paddler will often appear to escape from holes effortlessly.

■ Sticky, grabby holes are rarely overpowered, they are outsmarted.

It is no accident that a chapter on hands paddling should culminate a "how to" book on kayaking technique. When you have a paddle at your disposal, it is easy to overuse it and over depend on it . . . and never learn playboating essentials. Eliminating the paddle allows you to learn basic techniques in their purest form—it forces you to use the kayak as your principal means of control

It is an error to think of hands paddling as in some way an "ultimate" whitewater skill. For one thing, it's an excellent way to learn boat control at any skill level, beginner to expert. Experts can learn from difficult maneuvers in difficult settings, while beginners should limit themselves to simple maneuvers in ideal conditions. The other reason not to put hands paddling on some sort of pedestal is because you can do so much more with your paddle than without it.

Hands paddling is fun and challenging, but it does not offer the same control or safety as a paddle. There is little room for error doing a hands roll, and it is much less reliable than a paddle roll when hole playing. Never practice hands paddling anywhere you would feel uncomfortable swimming.

Drift practice (as described in chapter 11) while holding your paddle in reserve is essential to learning stability and balance on whitewater. When you can anticipate needed lean and edge control changes, and find yourself riding out even large edge tilts, you are ready to try hole playing without a paddle. A hands roll, although not essential if your buddy is waiting to bail you out, will markedly increase your self-confidence and make every maneuver easier to attempt.

The first thing to try is side-surfing a known and friendly hole. Paddle into a side-surf and test the hole using one hand to brace and the other to hold your paddle in reserve. When you feel comfortable, toss your paddle to a friend in a nearby eddy. You'll be surprised at how remarkably stable hands paddling can feel. When side-surfing, the best, least aerated water for bracing is the water your boat is sitting on, so your hands brace should usually be placed next to the boat's edge. Leaning forward will lower your center of gravity, making it easier to keep your weight over the boat, and also letting you use more of your hand and arm for support if needed. By leaning all the way forward, as in figure 17.1, you can rest comfortably on the forward deck and easily keep your balance.

A window shade while side-surfing is the easiest of maneuvers while hands paddling; just be sure you initiate the roll by quickly leaning

■ You'll be surprised at how remarkably stable hands paddling can feel.

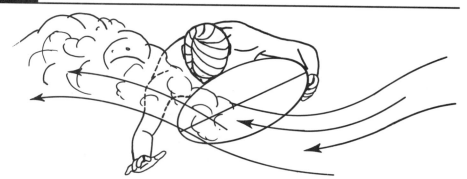

Figure 17.1: When side-surfing without a paddle, keep the hand and arm used for bracing near the boat's rail.

forward (figure 17.2). You want your head in close to the deck so that you don't hit any upstream obstructions with your head/helmet. Less obviously, you want to minimize drag so that you aren't pushed out of the hole during your roll. Don't worry about which hand to roll up with, let the current decide by pushing your body downstream and toward the surface. A gentle hipsnap will slide the kayak underneath you, and bring you back into a stable side-surf.

Hands paddling from an eddy into a hole or onto a wave is one of the more difficult things to do. There is little margin for error because directional control and forward power are minimal compared to that using a paddle. Develop good forward speed in the eddy to supply the momentum you'll need to carry your kayak across the eddy line. You've got to enter current at just the right angle when punching an eddy line, and enter onto a wave in precisely the right place. If you need to change

▪ You've got to enter current at just the right angle when punching an eddy line, and enter onto a wave in precisely the right place.

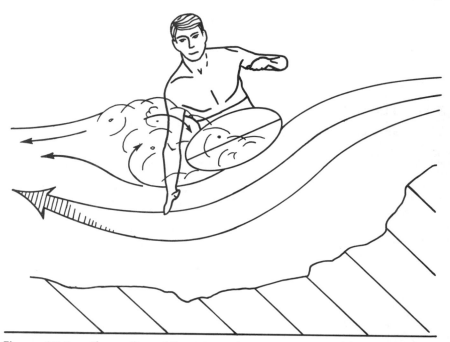

Figure 17.2 a: If you flip while side-surfing, the current will tell you which side to roll on. See figure 17.2 b-e on the following page.

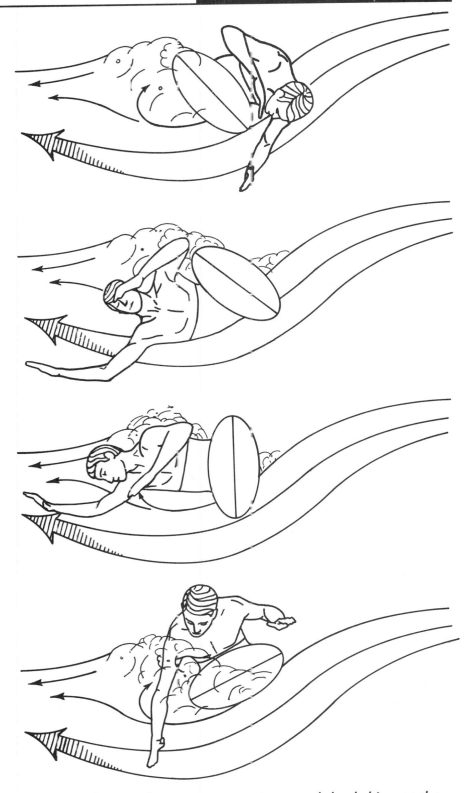

Figure 17.2 b-e: Let the current support you, and slowly hipsnap the boat in order to slide the kayak back underneath your body.

direction after punching the eddy line, you'll only be able to do so by ruddering with your hands (few people can hands paddle forward strongly enough to counteract the effects of current on the hull). This will add drag, slow the boat, and allow the current to blow you out of control.

Once on a wave, you'll find bow-surfing becomes a delicate business. Your ability to control the kayak's surfing angle is limited because your hands cannot direct the flow of current into or away from the boat as well as a paddle blade can. The tools available to you are edge control, fore and aft lean, forward and backward hand-strokes, and adding drag with hand and arm pressure on one or both sides of the kayak. It is difficult to compensate for any loss in surfing angle, so corrections must be made early while small inputs can still do the job.

■ It is difficult to compensate for any loss in surfing angle, so corrections must be made early while small inputs can still do the job.

One advantage you have is being able to use both hands to stroke with at the same time. Hand strokes on the upstream side of the boat are extremely useful except when side-surfing near the center of a hole. Here, you frequently can't reach the upstream water because your arm does not have the long reach of a paddle. Hands paddling gives you the unique ability to pivot the kayak on a pillow or the crest of a wave by paddling forward on one side and backward on the other.

If you flip while hands paddling, it's usually best to maintain the momentum of tipping over with an extremely rapid forward lean into the setup position. You can move much faster without being encumbered by a 6 to 7 foot-long paddle! Snap off your hands roll so that rolling upright is part of the same motion as rolling upside down. Your ability to lean forward into the setup position rapidly, even after missing a backward-leaning hands roll, is the reason I feel that your exposure to river hazards during a backward-leaning roll is no greater than with a forward-leaning one.

I've found that the effectiveness of forward-leaning and backward-leaning hands rolls, however, are not always equal; and that the reliability of your hands roll can vary tremendously in whitewater, depending upon whether you flip while bow-surfing or stern-surfing. To understand this, you need only know that the ability to hands roll upright depends on the amount of resistance to the current your trunk, arm, and hands can generate (purchase and platform are other terms I've used for this). A flip while bow-surfing allows you to catch the current in your arms and chest like a parachute opening when doing a forward-leaning roll (figure 17.3 a). The same roll after a flip stern-surfing is far less effective because your hands and your trunk are moving only toward the bow, the same direction as the current (figure 17.3 b). The current decreases your available purchase in this situation and saps the strength from a forward-leaning roll.

A backward-leaning hands roll, on the other hand, gives good

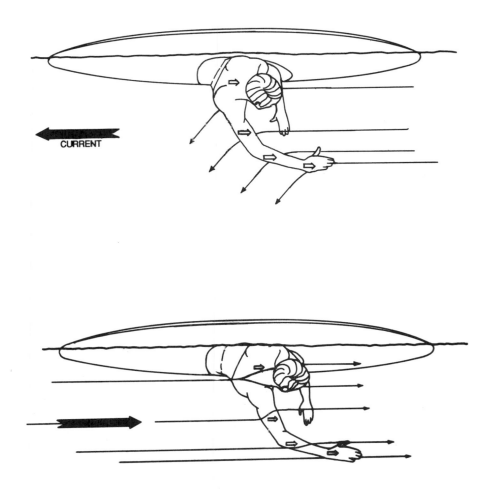

Figure 17.3 a,b: These drawings show the effect of current on your hands roll when leaning directly into the current (opposing it), and in the same direction as the current. The open arrows show the direction the body is moving, the closed arrows show the direction of the current. A A two-stroke, forward-leaning hands roll is highly effective leaning into the current. This situation would occur if you flipped while bow-surfing. Tremendous purchase is obtained as current encounters your chest, arm, and hand. B The same roll is much less effective after a flip stern-surfing.

purchase with the current flowing in either direction because you can sweep your hand and arm either forward or backward to oppose the current (figures 17.4 a and b). Most of the playboaters I see use a backward-leaning hands roll, and this is probably because they find it more reliable. I would definitely recommend using a backward-leaning roll following any flip where you had been facing downstream.

Hole escapes while hands paddling demand that you be able to

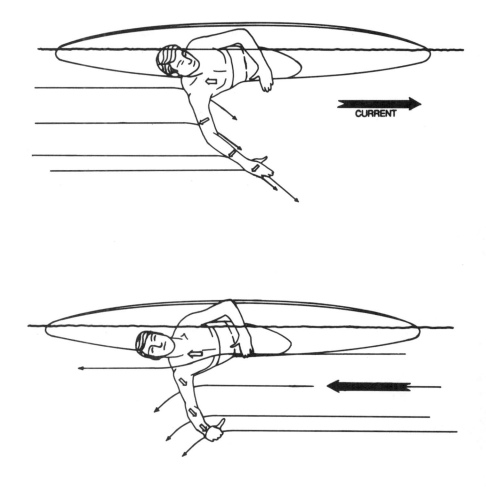

CURRENT

Figure 17.4 a,b: A two-stroke backward-leaning hands roll is effective with current flowing in either direction.

move your kayak strongly from side to side in the hole. You'll find backward hand-strokes are much more powerful than forward hand-strokes, so if you find yourself stuck in the hole, first move the kayak forward as far as you can. Then stroke strongly backward (on both sides of the boat when able, keeping your upstream edge raised). At the corners of the hole both hands can easily reach the water and can be used to power the boat onto the crest, or out of the hole entirely.

If you don't reach hole escape velocity sitting upright, you can try to escape upside down by leaning to the outside when you have moved backward as far toward the corner of the hole as you can. Place all the resistance to downstream current you possess, your entire upper body with extended arms, into the fast downstream-flowing current. This is probably your best bet for escaping a deep hole even though it means you'll escape upside-down, and then need to roll upright farther downstream.

This brief overview of hands paddling should help you get out there on a wave or in a hole and discover what works for you and your particular kayak. Good boat control will allow you to experiment with different techniques without losing stability and being knocked over. What you learn will have a far reaching effect on your paddling style, your self-confidence and your knowledge of whitewater. You can see the difference between two paddlers who can each do the same hole-playing maneuver using their paddles, but one of whom also practices hands paddling—the hands paddler will look smoother, and work less.

Conclusion

Much of my personal enjoyment of kayaking comes from analyzing the sport, as you may have already gathered. I am intrigued by questions like: Why do some people reliably roll their kayaks on flat water, but fail to on whitewater? If I can roll the kayak sweeping the paddle from bow to stern, couldn't I also roll it setting up with my head on the stern deck and sweeping the blade from stern to bow? (Yes, you can). Why do some paddlers feel one kayak is harder to roll than another? And most tantalizing of all, why can *he* or *she* do something that I can't?

I have great fun testing my solutions to these puzzles, especially when I paddle a kayak with a different volume or shape. I put my whole perspective of "how things work" out there to the test every time I get on the river. I have learned a great deal through this process, but I'm less impressed by my discoveries than I am by how frequently I have had to reassess, modify, or change my point of view.

Many river maneuvers that prove hard to learn or that continue to plague even advanced kayakers (for example combat rolls, or hole escapes) have a common underlying theme: an over-reliance on the paddle to compensate for poor boat control. This isn't surprising; the paddle is an obvious device for controlling the kayak, whereas good boat control is usually invisible to the observer. Throughout this book I've tried to heighten your awareness of how you can use your kayak to improve stability and balance, whether bracing or hole playing. You'll find it useful, just as I have, to question and test these ideas. By doing so, you'll more fully develop or modify your own perceptions of what works and what is good technique.

The river can't be controlled or subdued, and so all of us must learn how to move with it, to "go with the flow." Boating is logical, water follows natural laws, and the forces acting on you and your kayak, though immense, can be understood and used to your advantage. I hope this book has helped you to understand how edge control and balance enter the equation. Good boat control will help you paddle in harmony with the river, instead of struggling against it.

■ Many river maneuvers that prove hard to learn have a common underlying theme: an over-reliance on the paddle to compensate for poor boat control.

River Etiquette

River courtesy becomes important when you begin to spend a lot of time playboating, because you'll frequently be sharing your play spot with other paddlers. These unwritten rules of the river are "old hat" to experienced paddlers, but not to newcomers. When first learning to kayak, I was happy and relieved if I could "make" an eddy; I wasn't very concerned with how I made it, or with the other boats already there. I can remember a few times when I sat in an eddy getting psyched up to enter a wave or peel-out into really big water. When I went for it, I was shocked to find myself right in front of another paddler already in the current. Experience gives us the ability and confidence to look beyond the water immediately surrounding the kayak, and the obligation to become more responsible in our paddling. Here are a few guidelines.

1. The paddlers upstream in the current should be given the right of way, so if you are playing on a wave and a paddler or raft appears upstream from you, move off the wave and let them pass. Never pull out in front of another paddler in the current.

2. If you are paddling downstream and you see a paddler surfing downstream from you, pull off into an eddy, if possible, until he is done. That's courtesy, and it also gives you a shot at the same play spot.

3. When entering an eddy, do so above or below other paddlers, if possible, rather than right next to them. If there are boaters waiting in line to play a hole, eddy out below the last paddler in line.

4. It's OK to stop abruptly in a hole in midstream to surf or play, but not if there are other paddlers following immediately behind you. It is better to stop in an eddy upstream of your wave, and hop on it after the others have passed.

5. Use enough boat control in eddies and in the current not to jostle or spear other boaters.

6. Restrict your bow- or side-surf to a minute or two if other paddlers are waiting. It is far more impressive to do your stuff fast and clean and then leave with a satisfied smile, than it is to spend a long time "hogging" a wave or hole.

7. When any paddler needs assistance, immediately come to his aide if you have the skill to do so. Don't wait to see if someone else has that responsibility.

About the Author

Paul Dutky began kayaking while living in Tennessee, where he paddled widely throughout the southeast until moving into western Washington in 1988. Boating adventures have taken him to the Rocky mountain states, British Columbia, Costa Rica and Chile. He is an emergency medicine physician who lives in Bremerton, Washington.

Colophon

The text of this book was set in ITC Souvenir, an informal-style digital typeface noted for its rounded serifs. The display type was set in Optima. The book was designed by Frank Logue and composed by Carolina Graphics Group in Rome Georgia. The cover design is by Leslie Cummins, with a cover photo by Nicole Jones.